PENGUIN PLAYS
PL53
HEARTBREAK HOUSE

D1324820

BERNARD SHAW

HEARTBREAK HOUSE

A FANTASIA IN THE RUSSIAN
MANNER ON ENGLISH THEMES

PENGUIN BOOKS

Penguin Books Ltd, Harmondsworth, Middlesex, England
Penguin Books Australia Ltd, Ringwood, Victoria, Australia

—

First published 1919
This revised Standard Edition first published by Constable 1931
Published in Penguin Books 1964
Reprinted 1967, 1968

—

—

Made and printed in Great Britain
by Western Printing Services Ltd, Bristol
Set in Monotype Baskerville

CONTENTS

HEARTBREAK HOUSE AND HORSEBACK HALL   7
  Where Heartbreak House Stands   7
  The Inhabitants   8
  Horseback Hall   9
  Revolution on the Shelf   9
  The Cherry Orchard   10
  Nature's Long Credits   11
  The Wicked Half Century   12
  Hypochondria   14
  Those Who do not Know how to Live must
    Make a Merit of Dying   15
  War Delirium   16
  Madness in Court   17
  The Long Arm of War   19
  The Rabid Watchdogs of Liberty   20
  The Sufferings of the Sane   22
  Evil in the Throne of Good   24
  Straining at the Gnat and Swallowing the Camel 25
  Little Minds and Big Battles   27
  The Dumb Capables and the Noisy Incapables   28
  The Practical Business Men   30
  How the Fools Shouted the Wise Men Down   30
  The Mad Election   31
  The Yahoo and the Angry Ape   33
  Plague on Both your Houses!   34
  How the Theatre Fared   36
  The Soldier at the Theatre Front   37
  Commerce in the Theatre   39
  Unser Shakespear   39
  The Higher Drama put out of Action   40
  Church and Theatre   42
  The Next Phase   44
  The Ephemeral Thrones and the Eternal Theatre 46
  How War Muzzles the Dramatic Poet   47

HEARTBREAK HOUSE
AND HORSEBACK HALL

WHERE HEARTBREAK HOUSE STANDS

HEARTBREAK HOUSE is not merely the name of the play which follows this preface. It is cultured, leisured Europe before the war. When the play was begun not a shot had been fired; and only the professional diplomatists and the very few amateurs whose hobby is foreign policy even knew that the guns were loaded. A Russian playwright, Tchekov, had produced four fascinating dramatic studies of Heartbreak House, of which three, The Cherry Orchard, Uncle Vanya, and The Seagull, had been performed in England. Tolstoy, in his Fruits of Enlightenment, had shewn us through it in his most ferociously contemptuous manner. Tolstoy did not waste any sympathy on it: it was to him the house in which Europe was stifling its soul; and he knew that our utter enervation and futilization in that overheated drawing-room atmosphere was delivering the world over to the control of ignorant and soulless cunning and energy, with the frightful consequences which have now overtaken it. Tolstoy was no pessimist: he was not disposed to leave the house standing if he could bring it down about the ears of its pretty and amiable voluptuaries; and he wielded the pickaxe with a will. He treated the case of the inmates as one of opium poisoning, to be dealt with by seizing the patients roughly and exercising them violently until they were broad awake. Tchekov, more of a fatalist, had no faith in these charming people extricating themselves. They would, he thought, be sold up and sent adrift by the bailiffs; therefore he had no scruple in exploiting and even flattering their charm.

THE INHABITANTS

Tchekov's plays, being less lucrative than swings and round-abouts, got no further in England, where theatres are only ordinary commercial affairs, than a couple of performances by the Stage Society. We stared and said, 'How Russian!' They did not strike me in that way. Just as Ibsen's intensely Norwegian plays exactly fitted every middle and professional class suburb in Europe, these intensely Russian plays fitted all the country houses in Europe in which the pleasures of music, art, literature, and the theatre had supplanted hunting, shooting, fishing, flirting, eating and drinking. The same nice people, the same utter futility. The nice people could read; some of them could write; and they were the only repositories of culture who had social opportunities of contact with our politicians, administrators, and newspaper proprietors, or any chance of sharing or influencing their activities. But they shrank from that contact. They hated politics. They did not wish to realize Utopia for the common people: they wished to realize their favorite fictions and poems in their own lives; and, when they could, they lived without scruple on incomes which they did nothing to earn. The women in their girlhood made themselves look like variety theatre stars, and settled down later into the types of beauty imagined by the previous generation of painters. They took the only part of our society in which there was leisure for high culture, and made it an economic, political, and, as far as practicable, a moral vacuum; and as Nature, abhorring the vacuum, immediately filled it up with sex and with all sorts of refined pleasures, it was a very delightful place at its best for moments of relaxation. In other moments it was disastrous. For prime ministers and their like, it was a veritable Capua.

HORSEBACK HALL

But where were our front benchers to nest if not here? The alternative to Heartbreak House was Horseback Hall, consisting of a prison for horses with an annex for the ladies and gentlemen who rode them, hunted them, talked about them, bought them and sold them, and gave nine-tenths of their lives to them, dividing the other tenth between charity, churchgoing (as a substitute for religion), and conservative electioneering (as a substitute for politics). It is true that the two establishments got mixed at the edges. Exiles from the library, the music room, and the picture gallery would be found languishing among the stables, miserably discontented; and hardy horsewomen who slept at the first chord of Schumann were born, horribly misplaced, into the garden of Klingsor; but sometimes one came upon horsebreakers and heartbreakers who could make the best of both worlds. As a rule, however, the two were apart and knew little of one another; so the prime minister folk had to choose between barbarism and Capua. And of the two atmospheres it is hard to say which was the more fatal to statesmanship.

REVOLUTION ON THE SHELF

Heartbreak House was quite familiar with revolutionary ideas on paper. It aimed at being advanced and freethinking, and hardly ever went to church or kept the Sabbath except by a little extra fun at week-ends. When you spent a Friday to Tuesday in it you found on the shelf in your bedroom not only the books of poets and novelists, but of revolutionary biologists and even economists. Without at least a few plays by myself and Mr Granville Barker, and a few stories by Mr H. G. Wells, Mr Arnold Bennett, and Mr John Galsworthy, the house would have been out of the movement. You would find Blake among the poets, and beside him Bergson, Butler, Scott Haldane, the poems of Meredith and

9

Thomas Hardy, and, generally speaking, all the literary implements for forming the mind of the perfect modern Socialist and Creative Evolutionist. It was a curious experience to spend Sunday in dipping into these books, and on Monday morning to read in the daily paper that the country had just been brought to the verge of anarchy because a new Home Secretary or chief of police, without an idea in his head that his great-grandmother might not have had to apologize for, had refused to 'recognize' some powerful Trade Union, just as a gondola might refuse to recognize a 20,000-ton liner.

In short, power and culture were in separate compartments. The barbarians were not only literally in the saddle, but on the front bench in the House of Commons, with nobody to correct their incredible ignorance of modern thought and political science but upstarts from the counting-house, who had spent their lives furnishing their pockets instead of their minds. Both, however, were practised in dealing with money and with men, as far as acquiring the one and exploiting the other went; and although this is as undesirable an expertness as that of the medieval robber baron, it qualifies men to keep an estate or a business going in its old routine without necessarily understanding it, just as Bond Street tradesmen and domestic servants keep fashionable society going without any instruction in sociology.

THE CHERRY ORCHARD

The Heartbreak people neither could nor would do anything of the sort. With their heads as full of the Anticipations of Mr H. G. Wells as the heads of our actual rulers were empty even of the anticipations of Erasmus or Sir Thomas More, they refused the drudgery of politics, and would have made a very poor job of it if they had changed their minds. Not that they would have been allowed to meddle anyhow, as only through the accident of being a hereditary peer can anyone in these days of Votes for Everybody get into parliament if handicapped by a serious modern cultural equipment; but if they had, their habit of living in a vacuum would have left them helpless and ineffective in public affairs. Even in private life they were often helpless wasters of their inheritance, like the people in Tchekov's Cherry Orchard. Even those who lived within their incomes were really kept going by their solicitors and agents, being unable to manage an estate or run a business without continual prompting from those who have to learn how to do such things or starve.

From what is called Democracy no corrective to this state of things could be hoped. It is said that every people has the Government it deserves. It is more to the point that every Government has the electorate it deserves; for the orators of the front bench can edify or debauch an ignorant electorate at will. Thus our democracy moves in a vicious circle of reciprocal worthiness and unworthiness.

NATURE'S LONG CREDITS

Nature's way of dealing with unhealthy conditions is unfortunately not one that compels us to conduct a solvent hygiene on a cash basis. She demoralizes us with long credits and reckless overdrafts, and then pulls us up cruelly with catastrophic bankruptcies. Take, for example, common domestic sanitation. A whole city generation may neglect it utterly and scandalously, if not with absolute impunity, yet without any evil consequences that anyone thinks of tracing to it. In a hospital two generations of medical students may tolerate dirt and carelessness, and then go out into general practice to spread the doctrine that fresh air is a fad, and sanitation an imposture set up to make profits for plumbers. Then suddenly Nature takes her revenge. She strikes at the city with a pestilence and at the hospital with an epidemic of hospital gangrene, slaughtering right and left until the innocent young have paid for the guilty old, and the account is balanced. And then she goes to sleep again and gives another period of credit, with the same result.

This is what has just happened in our political hygiene. Political science has been as recklessly neglected by Governments and electorates during my lifetime as sanitary science was in the days of Charles the Second. In international relations diplomacy has been a boyishly lawless affair of family intrigues, commercial and territorial brigandage, torpors of pseudo-goodnature produced by laziness, and spasms of ferocious activity produced by terror. But in these islands we muddled through. Nature gave us a longer credit than she gave to France or Germany or Russia. To British centenarians who died in their beds in 1914, any dread of having to hide underground in London from the shells of an enemy seemed more remote and fantastic than a dread of the appearance of a colony of cobras and rattlesnakes in Kensington Gardens. In the prophetic works of Charles Dickens we were warned against many evils which have since come to pass; but of the evil of being slaughtered by a foreign foe on our own doorsteps there was no shadow. Nature gave us a very long credit; and we abused it to the utmost. But when she struck at last she struck with a vengeance. For four years she smote our firstborn and heaped on us plagues of which Egypt never dreamed. They were all as preventible as the great Plague of London, and came solely because they had not been prevented. They were not undone by winning the war. The earth is still bursting with the dead bodies of the victors.

THE WICKED HALF CENTURY

It is difficult to say whether indifference and neglect are worse than false doctrine; but Heartbreak House and Horseback Hall unfortunately suffered from both. For half a century before the war civilization had been going to the devil very precipitately under the influence of a pseudo-science as disastrous as the blackest Calvinism. Calvinism taught that as we are predestinately saved or damned, nothing that we do can alter our destiny. Still, as Calvinism gave the individual no clue as to whether he had drawn a lucky number or an unlucky one, it left him a fairly strong interest in encouraging his hopes of salvation and allaying his fear of damnation by behaving as one of the elect might be expected to behave rather than as one of the reprobate. But in the middle of the nineteenth century naturalists and physicists assured the world, in the name of Science, that salvation and damnation are all nonsense, and that predestination is the central truth of religion, inasmuch as human beings are produced by their environment, their sins and good deeds being only a series of chemical and mechanical reactions over which they have no control. Such figments as mind, choice, purpose, conscience, will, and so forth, are, they taught, mere illusions, produced because they are useful in the continual struggle of the human machine to maintain its environment in a favourable condition, a process incidentally involving the ruthless destruction or subjection of its competitors for the supply (assumed to be limited) of subsistence available. We taught Prussia this religion; and Prussia bettered our instruction so effectively that we presently found ourselves confronted with the necessity of destroying Prussia to prevent Prussia destroying us. And that has just ended in each destroying the other to an extent doubtfully reparable in our time.

It may be asked how so imbecile and dangerous a creed ever came to be accepted by intelligent beings. I will answer that question more fully in my next volume of plays, which will be entirely devoted to the subject. For the present I will only say that there were better reasons than the obvious one that such sham science as this opened a scientific career to very stupid men, and all the other careers to shameless rascals, provided they were industrious enough. It is true that this motive operated very powerfully; but when the new departure in scientific doctrine which is associated with the name of the great naturalist Charles Darwin began, it was not only a reaction against a barbarous pseudo-evangelical teleology intolerably obstructive to all scientific progress, but was accompanied, as it happened, by discoveries of extraordinary interest in physics, chemistry, and that lifeless method of evolution which its investigators called Natural Selection. Howbeit, there was only one result possible in the ethical sphere, and that was the banishment of conscience from human affairs, or, as Samuel Butler vehemently put it, 'of mind from the universe.'

HYPOCHONDRIA

Now Heartbreak House, with Butler and Bergson and Scott Haldane alongside Blake and the other major poets on its shelves (to say nothing of Wagner and the tone poets), was not so completely blinded by the doltish materialism of the laboratories as the uncultured world outside. But being an idle house it was a hypochondriacal house, always running after cures. It would stop eating meat, not on valid Shelleyan grounds, but in order to get rid of a bogey called Uric Acid; and it would actually let you pull all its teeth out to exorcize another demon named Pyorrhea. It was superstitious, and addicted to table-rapping, materialization séances, clairvoyance, palmistry, crystal-gazing and the like to such an extent that it may be doubted whether ever before in the history of the world did soothsayers, astrologers, and unregistered therapeutic specialists of all sorts flourish as they did during this half century of the drift to the abyss. The registered doctors and surgeons were hard put to it to compete with the unregistered. They were not clever enough to appeal to the imagination and sociability of the Heartbreakers by the arts of the actor, the orator, the poet, the winning conversationalist. They had to fall back coarsely on

the terror of infection and death. They prescribed inocula-
tions and operations. Whatever part of a human being could
be cut out without necessarily killing him they cut out; and
he often died (unnecessarily of course) in consequence. From
such trifles as uvulas and tonsils they went on to ovaries and
appendices until at last no one's inside was safe. They explained that the human intestine was too long, and that
nothing could make a child of Adam healthy except short
circuiting the pylorus by cutting a length out of the lower
intestine and fastening it directly to the stomach. As their
mechanist theory taught them that medicine was the business of the chemist's laboratory, and surgery of the carpenter's shop, and also that Science (by which they meant their
practices) was so important that no consideration for the
interests of any individual creature, whether frog or philosopher, much less the vulgar commonplaces of sentimental
ethics, could weigh for a moment against the remotest off-
chance of an addition to the body of scientific knowledge,
they operated and vivisected and inoculated and lied on a
stupendous scale, clamoring for and actually acquiring such
legal powers over the bodies of their fellow-citizens as neither
king, pope, nor parliament dare ever have claimed. The In-
quisition itself was a Liberal institution compared to the
General Medical Council.

THOSE WHO DO NOT KNOW HOW TO LIVE MUST
MAKE A MERIT OF DYING

Heartbreak House was far too lazy and shallow to extricate
itself from this palace of evil enchantment. It rhapsodized
about love; but it believed in cruelty. It was afraid of the
cruel people; and it saw that cruelty was at least effective.
Cruelty did things that made money, whereas Love did
nothing but prove the soundness of Larochefoucauld's saying that very few people would fall in love if they had never
read about it. Heartbreak House, in short, did not know

how to live, at which point all that was left to it was the boast that at least it knew how to die: a melancholy accomplishment which the outbreak of war presently gave it practically unlimited opportunities of displaying. Thus were the firstborn of Heartbreak House smitten; and the young, the innocent, the hopeful expiated the folly and worthlessness of their elders.

WAR DELIRIUM

Only those who have lived through a first-rate war, not in the field, but at home, and kept their heads, can possibly understand the bitterness of Shakespear and Swift, who both went through this experience. The horror of Peer Gynt in the madhouse, when the lunatics, exalted by illusions of splendid talent and visions of a dawning millennium, crowned him as their emperor, was tame in comparison. I do not know whether anyone really kept his head completely except those who had to keep it because they had to conduct the war at first hand. I should not have kept my own (as far as I did keep it) if I had not at once understood that as a scribe and speaker I too was under the most serious public obligation to keep my grip on realities; but this did not save me from a considerable degree of hyperaesthesia. There were of course some happy people to whom the war meant nothing: all political and general matters lying outside their little circle of interest. But the ordinary war-conscious civilian went mad, the main symptom being a conviction that the whole order of nature had been reversed. All foods, he felt, must now be adulterated. All schools must be closed. No advertisements must be sent to the newspapers, of which new editions must appear and be bought up every ten minutes. Travelling must be stopped, or, that being impossible, greatly hindered. All pretences about fine art and culture and the like must be flung off as an intolerable affectation; and the picture galleries and museums and schools at once occupied by war workers. The British Museum itself was saved only by a hairsbreadth. The sincerity of all this, and of much more which would not be believed if I chronicled it, may be established by one conclusive instance of the general craziness. Men were seized with the illusion that they could win the war by giving away money. And they not only subscribed millions to Funds of all sorts with no discoverable object, and to ridiculous voluntary organizations for doing what was plainly the business of the civil and military authorities, but actually handed out money to any thief in the street who had the presence of mind to pretend that he (or she) was 'collecting' it for the annihilation of the enemy. Swindlers were emboldened to take offices; label themselves Anti-Enemy Leagues; and simply pocket the money that was heaped on them. Attractively dressed young women found that they had nothing to do but parade the streets, collecting-box in hand, and live gloriously on the profits. Many months elapsed before, as a first sign of returning sanity, the police swept an Anti-Enemy secretary into prison *pour encourager les autres*, and the passionate penny collecting of the Flag Days was brought under some sort of regulation.

MADNESS IN COURT

The demoralization did not spare the Law Courts. Soldiers were acquitted, even on fully proved indictments for wilful murder, until at last the judges and magistrates had to announce that what was called the Unwritten Law, which meant simply that a soldier could do what he liked with impunity in civil life, was not the law of the land, and that a Victoria Cross did not carry with it a perpetual plenary indulgence. Unfortunately the insanity of the juries and magistrates did not always manifest itself in indulgence. No person unlucky enough to be charged with any sort of conduct, however reasonable and salutary, that did not smack of war delirium had the slightest chance of acquittal. There was in the country, too, a certain number of people who had conscientious objections to war as criminal or unchristian. The Act of Parliament introducing Compulsory Military Service thoughtlessly exempted these persons, merely requiring them to prove the genuineness of their convictions. Those who did so were very ill-advised from the point of view of their own personal interest; for they were persecuted with savage logicality in spite of the law; whilst those who made no pretence of having any objection to war at all, and had not only had military training in Officers' Training Corps, but had proclaimed on public occasions that they were perfectly ready to engage in civil war on behalf of their political opinions, were allowed the benefit of the Act on the ground that they did not approve of this particular war. For the Christians there was no mercy. In cases where the evidence as to their being killed by ill treatment was so unequivocal that the verdict would certainly have been one of wilful murder had the prejudice of the coroner's jury been on the other side, their tormentors were gratuitously declared to be blameless. There was only one virtue, pugnacity: only one vice, pacifism. That is an essential condition of war; but the Government had not the courage to legislate accordingly; and its law was set aside for Lynch law.

The climax of legal lawlessness was reached in France. The greatest Socialist statesman in Europe, Jaurès, was shot and killed by a gentleman who resented his efforts to avert the war. M. Clemenceau was shot by another gentleman of less popular opinions, and happily came off no worse than having to spend a precautionary couple of days in bed. The slayer of Jaurès was recklessly acquitted: the would-be slayer of M. Clemenceau was carefully found guilty. There is no reason to doubt that the same thing would have happened in England if the war had begun with a successful attempt to assassinate Keir Hardie, and ended with an unsuccessful one to assassinate Mr Lloyd George.

THE LONG ARM OF WAR

The pestilence which is the usual accompaniment of war was called influenza. Whether it was really a war pestilence or not was made doubtful by the fact that it did its worst in places remote from the battle-fields, notably on the west coast of North America and in India. But the moral pestilence, which was unquestionably a war pestilence, reproduced this phenomenon. One would have supposed that the war fever would have raged most furiously in the countries actually under fire, and that the others would be more reasonable. Belgium and Flanders, where over large districts literally not one stone was left upon another as the opposed armies drove each other back and forward over it after terrific preliminary bombardments, might have been pardoned for relieving their feelings more emphatically than by shrugging their shoulders and saying '*C'est la guerre.*' England, inviolate for so many centuries that the swoop of war on her homesteads had long ceased to be more credible than a return of the Flood, could hardly be expected to keep her temper sweet when she knew at last what it was to hide in cellars and underground railway stations, or lie quaking in bed, whilst bombs crashed, houses crumbled, and aircraft guns distributed shrapnel on friend and foe alike until certain shop windows in London, formerly full of fashionable hats, were filled with steel helmets. Slain and mutilated women and children, and burnt and wrecked dwellings, excuse a good deal of violent language, and produce a wrath on which many suns go down before it is appeased. Yet it was in the United States of America, where nobody slept the worse for the war, that the war fever went beyond all sense and reason. In European Courts there was vindictive illegality: in American Courts there was raving lunacy.

It is not for me to chronicle the extravagances of an Ally: let some candid American do that. I can only say that to us sitting in our gardens in England, with the guns in France making themselves felt by a throb in the air as unmistakeable as an audible sound, or with tightening hearts studying the phases of the moon in London in their bearing on the chances whether our houses would be standing or ourselves alive next morning, the newspaper accounts of the sentences American Courts were passing on young girls and old men alike for the expression of opinions which were being uttered amid thundering applause before huge audiences in England, and the more private records of the methods by which the American War Loans were raised, were so amazing that they would put the guns and the possibilities of a raid clean out of our heads for the moment.

THE RABID WATCHDOGS OF LIBERTY

Not content with these rancorous abuses of the existing law, the war maniacs made a frantic rush to abolish all constitutional guarantees of liberty and well-being. The ordinary law was superseded by Acts under which newspapers were seized and their printing machinery destroyed by simple police raids *à la Russe*, and persons arrested and shot without any pretence of trial by jury or publicity of procedure or evidence. Though it was urgently necessary that production should be increased by the most scientific organization and economy of labor, and though no fact was better established than that excessive duration and intensity of toil reduces production heavily instead of increasing it, the factory laws were suspended, and men and women recklessly overworked until the loss of their efficiency became too glaring to be ignored. Remonstrances and warnings were met either with an accusation of pro-Germanism or the formula, 'Remember that we are at war now.' I have said that men assumed that war had reversed the order of nature, and that all was lost unless we did the exact opposite of everything we had found necessary and beneficial in peace. But the truth was worse than that. The war did not change men's minds in any such impossible way. What really happened was that the impact of physical death and destruction, the one reality that every fool can understand, tore off the masks of education, art, science, and religion from our ignorance and barbarism, and left us glorying grotesquely in the licence suddenly accorded to our vilest passions and most abject terrors. Ever since Thucydides wrote his history, it has been on record that when the angel of death sounds his trumpet the pretences of civilization are blown from men's heads into the mud like hats in a gust of wind. But when this scripture was fulfilled among us, the shock was not the less appalling because a few students of Greek history were not surprised by it. Indeed these students threw themselves into the orgy as shamelessly as the illiterate. The Christian priest joining in the war dance without even throwing off his cassock first, and the respectable school governor expelling the German professor with insult and bodily violence, and declaring that no English child should ever again be taught the language of Luther and Goethe, were kept in countenance by the most impudent repudiations of every decency of civilization and every lesson of political experience on the part of the very persons who, as university professors, historians, philosophers, and men of science, were the accredited custodians of culture. It was crudely natural, and perhaps necessary for recruiting purposes, that German militarism and German dynastic ambition should be painted by journalists and recruiters in black and red as European dangers (as in fact they are), leaving it to be inferred that our own militarism and our own political constitution are millennially democratic (which they certainly are not); but when it came to frantic denunciations of German chemistry, German biology, German poetry, German music, German literature, German philosophy, and even German engineering, as malignant abominations standing towards British and French chemistry and so forth in the relation of heaven to hell, it was clear that the utterers of such barbarous ravings had never really understood or cared for the arts and sciences they professed and were profaning, and were only the appallingly degenerate descendants of the men of the seventeenth and eighteenth centuries who, recognizing no national frontiers in the great realm of the human mind, kept the European comity of that realm loftily and even ostentatiously above the rancors of the battle-field. Tearing the Garter from the Kaiser's leg, striking the German dukes from the roll of our peerage, changing the King's illustrious and historically appropriate surname for that of a traditionless locality, was not a very dignified business; but the erasure of German names from the British rolls of science and learning was a confession that in England the little respect paid to science and learning is only an affectation which hides a savage contempt for both. One felt that the figure of St George and the Dragon on our coinage should be replaced by that of the soldier driving his spear through Archimedes. But by that time there was no coinage: only paper money in which ten shillings called itself a pound as confidently as the people who were disgracing their country called themselves patriots.

THE SUFFERINGS OF THE SANE

The mental distress of living amid the obscene din of all these carmagnoles and corobberies was not the only burden that lay on sane people during the war. There was also the emotional strain, complicated by the offended economic sense, produced by the casualty lists. The stupid, the selfish, the narrow-minded, the callous and unimaginative were spared a great deal. 'Blood and destruction shall be so in use that mothers shall but smile when they behold their infants quartered by the hands of war,' was a Shakespearean prophecy that very nearly came true; for when nearly every house had a slaughtered son to mourn, we should all have gone quite out of our senses if we had taken our own and our friends' bereavements at their peace value. It became necessary to give them a false value; to proclaim the young life worthily and gloriously sacrificed to redeem the liberty of mankind, instead of to expiate the heedlessness and folly of their fathers, and expiate it in vain. We had even to assume that the parents and not the children had made the sacrifice, until at last the comic papers were driven to satirize fat old men, sitting comfortably in club chairs, and boasting of the sons they had 'given' to their country.

No one grudged these anodynes to acute personal grief; but they only embittered those who knew that the young men were having their teeth set on edge because their parents had eaten sour political grapes. Then think of the young men themselves! Many of them had no illusions about the policy that led to the war: they went clear-sighted to a horribly repugnant duty. Men essentially gentle and essentially wise, with really valuable work in hand, laid it down voluntarily and spent months forming fours in the barrack yard, and stabbing sacks of straw in the public eye, so that they might go out to kill and maim men as gentle as themselves. These men, who were perhaps, as a class, our most efficient soldiers (Frederick Keeling, for example), were not duped for a moment by the hypocritical melodrama that consoled and stimulated the others. They left their creative work to drudge at destruction, exactly as they would have left it to take their turn at the pumps in a sinking ship. They did not, like some of the conscientious objectors, hold back because the ship had been neglected by its officers and scuttled by its wreckers. The ship had to be saved, even if Newton had to leave his fluxions and Michael Angelo his marbles to save it; so they threw away the tools of

23

their beneficent and ennobling trades, and took up the bloodstained bayonet and the murderous bomb, forcing themselves to pervert their divine instinct for perfect artistic execution to the effective handling of these diabolical things, and their economic faculty for organization to the contriving of ruin and slaughter. For it gave an ironic edge to their tragedy that the very talents they were forced to prostitute made the prostitution not only effective, but even interesting; so that some of them were rapidly promoted, and found themselves actually becoming artists in war, with a growing relish for it, like Napoleon and all the other scourges of mankind, in spite of themselves. For many of them there was not even this consolation. They 'stuck it,' and hated it, to the end.

EVIL IN THE THRONE OF GOOD

This distress of the gentle was so acute that those who shared it in civil life, without having to shed blood with their own hands, or witness destruction with their own eyes, hardly cared to obtrude their own woes. Nevertheless, even when sitting at home in safety, it was not easy for those who had to write and speak about the war to throw away their highest conscience, and deliberately work to a standard of inevitable evil instead of to the ideal of life more abundant. I can answer for at least one person who found the change from the wisdom of Jesus and St Francis to the morals of Richard III and the madness of Don Quixote extremely irksome. But that change had to be made; and we are all the worse for it, except those for whom it was not really a change at all, but only a relief from hypocrisy.

Think, too, of those who, though they had neither to write nor to fight, and had no children of their own to lose, yet knew the inestimable loss to the world of four years of the life of a generation wasted on destruction. Hardly one of the epoch-making works of the human mind might not have been aborted or destroyed by taking their authors away from their natural work for four critical years. Not only were Shakespears and Platos being killed outright; but many of the best harvests of the survivors had to be sown in the barren soil of the trenches. And this was no mere British consideration. To the truly civilized man, to the good European, the slaughter of the German youth was as disastrous as the slaughter of the English. Fools exulted in 'German losses.' They were our losses as well. Imagine exulting in the death of Beethoven because Bill Sykes dealt him his death blow!

STRAINING AT THE GNAT AND SWALLOWING THE CAMEL

But most people could not comprehend these sorrows. There was a frivolous exultation in death for its own sake, which was at bottom an inability to realize that the deaths were real deaths and not stage ones. Again and again, when an air raider dropped a bomb which tore a child and its mother limb from limb, the people who saw it, though they had been reading with great cheerfulness of thousands of such happenings day after day in their newspapers, suddenly burst into furious imprecations on 'the Huns' as murderers, and shrieked for savage and satisfying vengeance. At such moments it became clear that the deaths they had not seen meant no more to them than the mimic deaths of the cinema screen. Sometimes it was not necessary that death should be actually witnessed: it had only to take place under circumstances of sufficient novelty and proximity to bring it home almost as sensationally and effectively as if it had been actually visible.

For example, in the spring of 1915 there was an appalling slaughter of our young soldiers at Neuve Chapelle and at the Gallipoli landing. I will not go so far as to say that our civilians were delighted to have such exciting news to read at breakfast. But I cannot pretend that I noticed either in the papers, or in general intercourse, any feeling beyond the usual one that the cinema show at the front was going splendidly, and that our boys were the bravest of the brave. Suddenly there came the news that an Atlantic liner, the Lusitania, had been torpedoed, and that several well-known first class passengers, including a famous theatrical manager and the author of a popular farce, had been drowned, among others. The others included Sir Hugh Lane; but as he had only laid the country under great obligations in the sphere of the fine arts, no great stress was laid on that loss.

Immediately an amazing frenzy swept through the country. Men who up to that time had kept their heads now lost them utterly. 'Killing saloon passengers! What next?' was the essence of the whole agitation; but it is far too trivial a phrase to convey the faintest notion of the rage which possessed us. To me, with my mind full of the hideous cost of Neuve Chapelle, Ypres, and the Gallipoli landing, the fuss about the Lusitania seemed almost a heartless impertinence, though I was well acquainted personally with the three best-known victims, and understood, better perhaps than most people, the misfortune of the death of Lane. I even found a grim satisfaction, very intelligible to all soldiers, in the fact that the civilians who found the war such splendid British sport should get a sharp taste of what it was to the actual combatants. I expressed my impatience very freely, and found that my very straightforward and natural feeling in the matter was received as a monstrous and heartless paradox. When I asked those who gaped at me whether they had anything to say about the holocaust of Festubert, they gaped wider than before, having totally forgotten it, or rather, having never realized it. They were not heartless any more than I was; but the big catastrophe was too big for them to grasp, and the little one had been just the right size for them. I was not surprised. Have I not seen a public body for just the same reason pass a vote for £30,000 without a word, and then spend three special meetings, prolonged into the night, over an item of seven shillings for refreshments?

LITTLE MINDS AND BIG BATTLES

Nobody will be able to understand the vagaries of public feeling during the war unless they bear constantly in mind that the war in its entire magnitude did not exist for the average civilian. He could not conceive even a battle, much less a campaign. To the suburbs the war was nothing but a suburban squabble. To the miner and navvy it was only a series of bayonet fights between German champions and English ones. The enormity of it was quite beyond most of us. Its episodes had to be reduced to the dimensions of a railway accident or a shipwreck before it could produce any effect on our minds at all. To us the ridiculous bombardments of Scarborough and Ramsgate were colossal tragedies, and the battle of Jutland a mere ballad. The words 'after thorough artillery preparation' in the news from the front meant nothing to us; but when our seaside trippers learned that an elderly gentleman at breakfast in a week-end marine hotel had been interrupted by a bomb dropping into his egg-cup, their wrath and horror knew no bounds. They declared that this would put a new spirit into the army, and had no suspicion that the soldiers in the trenches roared with laughter over it for days, and told each other that it would do the blighters at home good to have a taste of what the army was up against. Sometimes the smallness of view was pathetic. A man would work at home regardless of the call 'to make the world safe for democracy.' His brother would be killed at the front. Immediately he would throw up his work and take up the war as a family blood feud against the Germans. Sometimes it was comic. A wounded man, en-titled to his discharge, would return to the trenches with a grim determination to find the Hun who had wounded him and pay him out for it.

It is impossible to estimate what proportion of us, in khaki or out of it, grasped the war and its political antecedents as a whole in the light of any philosophy of history or knowledge of what war is. I doubt whether it was as high as our proportion of higher mathematicians. But there can be no doubt that it was prodigiously outnumbered by the comparatively ignorant and childish. Remember that these people had to be stimulated to make the sacrifices demanded by the war, and that this could not be done by appeals to a knowledge which they did not possess, and a comprehension of which they were incapable. When the armistice at last set me free to tell the truth about the war at the following general election, a soldier said to a candidate whom I was supporting 'If I had known all that in 1914, they would never have got me into khaki.' And that, of course, was precisely why it had been necessary to stuff him with a romance that any diplomatist would have laughed at. Thus the natural confusion of ignorance was increased by a deliberately propagated confusion of nursery bogey stories and melodramatic nonsense, which at last overreached itself and made it impossible to stop the war before we had not only achieved the triumph of vanquishing the German army and thereby overthrowing its militarist monarchy, but made the very serious mistake of ruining the centre of Europe, a thing that no sane European State could afford to do.

THE DUMB CAPABLES AND THE NOISY INCAPABLES

Confronted with this picture of insensate delusion and folly, the critical reader will immediately counterplead that England all this time was conducting a war which involved the organization of several millions of fighting men and of the workers who were supplying them with provisions, munitions, and transport, and that this could not have been done by a mob of hysterical ranters. This is fortunately true. To pass from the newspaper offices and political platforms and club fenders and suburban drawing-rooms to the Army and the munition factories was to pass from Bedlam to the busiest and sanest of workaday worlds. It was to rediscover England, and find solid ground for the faith of those who still believed in her. But a necessary condition of this efficiency was that those who were efficient should give all their time to their business and leave the rabble raving to its heart's content. Indeed the raving was useful to the efficient, because, as it was always wide of the mark, it often distracted attention very conveniently from operations that would have been defeated or hindered by publicity. A precept which I endeavored vainly to popularize early in the war, 'If you have anything to do go and do it: if not, for heaven's sake get out of the way,' was only half carried out. Certainly the capable people went and did it; but the incapables would by no means get out of the way: they fussed and bawled and were only prevented from getting very seriously into the way by the blessed fact that they never knew where the way was. Thus whilst all the efficiency of England was silent and invisible, all its imbecility was deafening the heavens with its clamor and blotting out the sun with its dust. It was also unfortunately intimidating the Government by its bluster-ings into using the irresistible powers of the State to intimi-date the sensible people, thus enabling a despicable minority of would-be lynchers to set up a reign of terror which could at any time have been broken by a single stern word from a responsible minister. But our ministers had not that sort of courage: neither Heartbreak House nor Horseback Hall had bred it, much less the suburbs. When matters at last came to the looting of shops by criminals under patriotic pretexts, it was the police force and not the Government that put its foot down. There was even one deplorable moment, during the submarine scare, in which the Government yielded to a childish cry for the maltreatment of naval prisoners of war, and, to our great disgrace, was forced by the enemy to behave itself. And yet behind all this public blundering and misconduct and futile mischief, the effective England was carrying on with the most formidable capacity and activity. The ostensible England was making the empire sick with its incontinences, its ignorances, its ferocities, its panics, and its endless and intolerable blarings of Allied national anthems in season and out. The esoteric England was proceeding irresistibly to the conquest of Europe.

THE PRACTICAL BUSINESS MEN

From the beginning the useless people set up a shriek for 'practical business men.' By this they meant men who had become rich by placing their personal interests before those of the country, and measuring the success of every activity by the pecuniary profit it brought to them and to those on whom they depended for their supplies of capital. The pitiable failure of some conspicuous samples from the first batch we tried of these poor devils helped to give the whole public side of the war an air of monstrous and hopeless farce. They proved not only that they were useless for public work, but that in a well-ordered nation they would never have been allowed to control private enterprise.

HOW THE FOOLS SHOUTED THE WISE MEN DOWN

Thus, like a fertile country flooded with mud, England shewed no sign of her greatness in the days when she was putting forth all her strength to save herself from the worst consequences of her littleness. Most of the men of action, occupied to the last hour of their time with urgent practical work, had to leave to idler people, or to professional rhetoricians, the presentation of the war to the reason and imagination of the country and the world in speeches, poems, manifestos, picture posters, and newspaper articles. I have had the privilege of hearing some of our ablest commanders talking about their work; and I have shared the common lot of reading the accounts of that work given to the world by the newspapers. No two experiences could be more different. But in the end the talkers obtained a dangerous ascendancy over the rank and file of the men of action; for though the great men of action are always inveterate talkers and often very clever writers, and therefore cannot have their minds formed for them by others, the average man of action, like the average fighter with the bayonet, can give no account of himself in words even to himself, and is apt to pick up and accept what he reads about himself and other people in the papers, except when the writer is rash enough to commit himself on technical points. It was not uncommon during the war to hear a soldier, or a civilian engaged on war work, describing events within his own experience that reduced to utter absurdity the ravings and maunderings of his daily paper, and yet echo the opinions of that paper like a parrot. Thus, to escape from the prevailing confusion and folly it was not enough to seek the company of the ordinary man of action: one had to get into contact with the master spirits. This was a privilege which only a handful of people could enjoy. For the unprivileged citizen there was no escape. To him the whole country seemed mad, futile, silly, incompetent, with no hope of victory except the hope that the enemy might be just as mad. Only by very resolute reflection and reasoning could he reassure himself that if there was nothing more solid beneath these appalling appearances the war could not possibly have gone on for a single day without a total breakdown of its organization.

THE MAD ELECTION

Happy were the fools and the thoughtless men of action in those days. The worst of it was that the fools were very strongly represented in parliament, as fools not only elect fools, but can persuade men of action to elect them too. The election that immediately followed the armistice was perhaps the maddest that has ever taken place. Soldiers who had done voluntary and heroic service in the field were defeated by persons who had apparently never run a risk or spent a farthing that they could avoid, and who even had in the course of the election to apologize publicly for bawling Pacifist or Pro-German at their opponent. Party leaders seek such followers, who can always be depended on to walk tamely into the lobby at the party whip's orders, provided the leader will make their seats safe for them by the process which was called, in derisive reference to the war rationing system, 'giving them the coupon.' Other incidents were so grotesque that I cannot mention them without enabling the reader to identify the parties, which would not be fair, as they were no more to blame than thousands of others who must necessarily be nameless. The general result was patently absurd; and the electorate, disgusted at its own work, instantly recoiled to the opposite extreme, and cast out all the coupon candidates at the earliest bye-elections by equally silly majorities. But the mischief of the general election could not be undone; and the Government had not only to pretend to abuse its European victory as it had promised, but actually to do it by starving the enemies who had thrown down their arms. It had, in short, won the election by pledging itself to be thriftlessly wicked, cruel, and vindictive; and it did not find it as easy to escape from this pledge as it had from nobler ones. The end, as I write, is not yet; but it is clear that this thoughtless savagery will recoil on the heads of the Allies so severely that we shall be forced by the sternest necessity to take up our share of healing the Europe we have wounded almost to death instead of attempting to complete her destruction.

THE YAHOO AND THE ANGRY APE

Contemplating this picture of a state of mankind so recent that no denial of its truth is possible, one understands Shakespear comparing Man to an angry ape, Swift describing him as a Yahoo rebuked by the superior virtue of the horse, and Wellington declaring that the British can behave themselves neither in victory nor defeat. Yet none of the three had seen war as we have seen it. Shakespear blamed great men, saying that 'Could great men thunder as Jove himself does Jove would ne'er be quiet; for every pelting petty officer would use his heaven for thunder: nothing but thunder.' What would Shakespear have said if he had seen something far more destructive than thunder in the hand of every village laborer, and found on the Messines Ridge the craters of the nineteen volcanoes that were let loose there at the touch of a finger that might have been a child's finger without the result being a whit less ruinous? Shakespear may have seen a Stratford cottage struck by one of Jove's thunderbolts, and have helped to extinguish the lighted thatch and clear away the bits of the broken chimney. What would he have said if he had seen Ypres as it is now, or returned to Stratford, as French peasants are returning to their homes today, to find the old familiar signpost inscribed 'To Stratford, 1 mile,' and at the end of the mile nothing but some holes in the ground and a fragment of a broken churn here and there? Would not the spectacle of the angry ape endowed with powers of destruction that Jove never pretended to, have beggared even his command of words?

And yet, what is there to say except that war puts a strain on human nature that breaks down the better half of it, and makes the worse half a diabolical virtue? Better for us if it broke it down altogether; for then the warlike way out of our difficulties would be barred to us, and we should take greater care not to get into them. In truth, it is, as Byron said, 'not difficult to die,' and enormously difficult to live: that explains why, at bottom, peace is not only better than war, but infinitely more arduous. Did any hero of the war face the glorious risk of death more bravely than the traitor Bolo faced the ignominious certainty of it? Bolo taught us all how to die: can we say that he taught us all how to live? Hardly a week passes now without some soldier who braved death in the field so recklessly that he was decorated or specially commended for it, being haled before our magistrates for having failed to resist the paltriest temptations of peace, with no better excuse than the old one that 'a man must live.' Strange that one who, sooner than do honest work, will sell his honor for a bottle of wine, a visit to the theatre, and an hour with a strange woman, all obtained by passing a worthless cheque, could yet stake his life on the most desperate chances of the battle-field! Does it not seem as if, after all, the glory of death were cheaper than the glory of life? If it is not easier to attain, why do so many more men attain it? At all events it is clear that the kingdom of the Prince of Peace has not yet become the kingdom of this world. His attempts at invasion have been resisted far more fiercely than the Kaiser's. Successful as that resistance has been, it has piled up a sort of National Debt that is not the less oppressive because we have no figures for it and do not intend to pay it. A blockade that cuts off 'the grace of our Lord' is in the long run less bearable than the blockades which merely cut off raw materials; and against that blockade our Armada is impotent. In the blockader's house, he has assured us, there are many mansions; but I am afraid they do not include either Heartbreak House or Horseback Hall.

PLAGUE ON BOTH YOUR HOUSES!

Meanwhile the Bolshevist picks and petards are at work on the foundations of both buildings; and though the Bolshevists may be buried in the ruins, their deaths will not save the edifices. Unfortunately they can be built again. Like Doubting Castle, they have been demolished many times by successive Greathearts, and rebuilt by Simple, Sloth, and Presumption, by Feeble Mind and Much Afraid, and by all the jurymen of Vanity Fair. Another generation of 'secondary education' at our ancient public schools and the cheaper institutions that ape them will be quite sufficient to keep the two going until the next war.

For the instruction of that generation I leave these pages as a record of what civilian life was during the war: a matter on which history is usually silent. Fortunately it was a very short war. It is true that the people who thought it could not last more than six months were very signally refuted by the event. As Sir Douglas Haig has pointed out, its Waterloos lasted months instead of hours. But there would have been nothing surprising in its lasting thirty years. If it had not been for the fact that the blockade achieved the amazing feat of starving out Europe, which it could not possibly have done had Europe been properly organized for war, or even for peace, the war would have lasted until the belligerents were so tired of it that they could no longer be compelled to compel themselves to go on with it. Considering its magnitude, the war of 1914–18 will certainly be classed as the shortest in history. The end came so suddenly that the combatants literally stumbled over it; and yet it came a full year later than it should have come if the belligerents had not been far too afraid of one another to face the situation sensibly. Germany, having failed to provide for the war she began, failed again to surrender before she was dangerously exhausted. Her opponents, equally improvident, went as much too close to bankruptcy as Germany to starvation. It was a bluff at which both were bluffed. And, with the usual irony of war, it remains doubtful whether Germany and Russia, the defeated, will not be the gainers; for the victors are already busy fastening on themselves the chains they have struck from the limbs of the vanquished.

HOW THE THEATRE FARED

Let us now contract our view rather violently from the European theatre of war to the theatre in which the fights are sham fights, and the slain, rising the moment the curtain has fallen, go comfortably home to supper after washing off their rosepink wounds. It is nearly twenty years since I was last obliged to introduce a play in the form of a book for lack of an opportunity of presenting it in its proper mode by a performance in a theatre. The war has thrown me back on this expedient. Heartbreak House has not yet reached the stage. I have withheld it because the war has completely upset the economic conditions which formerly enabled serious drama to pay its way in London. The change is not in the theatres nor in the management of them, nor in the authors and actors, but in the audiences. For four years the London theatres were crowded every night with thousands of soldiers on leave from the front. These soldiers were not seasoned London playgoers. A childish experience of my own gave me a clue to their condition. When I was a small boy I was taken to the opera. I did not then know what an opera was, though I could whistle a good deal of opera music. I had seen in my mother's album photographs of all the great opera singers, mostly in evening dress. In the theatre I found myself before a gilded balcony filled with persons in evening dress whom I took to be the opera singers. I picked out one massive dark lady as Alboni, and wondered how soon she would stand up and sing. I was puzzled by the fact that I was made to sit with my back to the singers instead of facing them. When the curtain went up, my astonishment and delight were unbounded.

THE SOLDIER AT THE THEATRE FRONT

In 1915 I saw in the theatres men in khaki in just the same predicament. To everyone who had my clue to their state of mind it was evident that they had never been in a theatre before and did not know what it was. At one of our great variety theatres I sat beside a young officer, not at all a rough specimen, who, even when the curtain rose and enlightened him as to the place where he had to look for his entertainment, found the dramatic part of it utterly incomprehensible. He did not know how to play his part of the game. He could understand the people on the stage singing and dancing and performing gymnastic feats. He not only understood but intensely enjoyed an artist who imitated cocks crowing and pigs squeaking. But the people who pretended that they were somebody else, and that the painted picture behind them was real, bewildered him. In his presence I realized how very sophisticated the natural man has to become before the conventions of the theatre can be easily acceptable, or the purpose of the drama obvious to him.

Well, from the moment when the routine of leave for our soldiers was established, such novices, accompanied by damsels (called flappers) often as innocent as themselves, crowded the theatres to the doors. It was hardly possible at first to find stuff crude enough to nurse them on. The best music-hall comedians ransacked their memories for the oldest quips and the most childish antics to avoid carrying the military spectators out of their depth. I believe that this was a mistake as far as the novices were concerned. Shakespear, or the dramatized histories of George Barnwell, Maria Martin, or the Demon Barber of Fleet Street, would probably have been quite popular with them. But the novices were only a minority after all. The cultivated soldier, who in time of peace would look at nothing theatrical except the most advanced

37

post-Ibsen plays in the most artistic settings, found himself, to his own astonishment, thirsting for silly jokes, dances, and brainlessly sensuous exhibitions of pretty girls. The author of some of the most grimly serious plays of our time told me that after enduring the trenches for months without a glimpse of the female of his species, it gave him an entirely innocent but delightful pleasure merely to see a flapper. The reaction from the battle-field produced a condition of hyperaesthesia in which all the theatrical values were altered. Trivial things gained intensity and stale things novelty. The actor, instead of having to coax his audiences out of the boredom which had driven them to the theatre in an ill humor to seek some sort of distraction, had only to exploit the bliss of smiling men who were no longer under fire and under military discipline, but actually clean and comfortable and in a mood to be pleased with anything and everything that a bevy of pretty girls and a funny man, or even a bevy of girls pretending to be pretty and a man pretending to be funny, could do for them.

Then could be seen every night in the theatres old-fashioned farcical comedies, in which a bedroom, with four doors on each side and a practicable window in the middle, was understood to resemble exactly the bedroom in the flats beneath and above, all three inhabited by couples consumed with jealousy. When these people came home drunk at night; mistook their neighbors' flats for their own; and in due course got into the wrong beds, it was not only the novices who found the resulting complications and scandals exquisitely ingenious and amusing, nor their equally verdant flappers who could not help squealing in a manner that astonished the oldest performers when the gentleman who had just come in drunk through the window pretended to undress, and allowed glimpses of his naked person to be descried from time to time. Men who had just read the news that Charles Wyndham was dying, and were thereby sadly reminded of Pink Dominos and the torrent of farcical comedies that followed it in his heyday until every trick of that trade had become so stale that the laughter they provoked turned to loathing: these veterans also, when they returned from the field, were as much pleased by what they knew to be stale and foolish as the novices by what they thought fresh and clever.

COMMERCE IN THE THEATRE

Wellington said that an army moves on its belly. So does a London theatre. Before a man acts he must eat. Before he performs plays he must pay rent. In London we have no theatres for the welfare of the people: they are all for the sole purpose of producing the utmost obtainable rent for the proprietor. If the twin flats and twin beds produce a guinea more than Shakespear, out goes Shakespear, and in come the twin flats and the twin beds. If the brainless bevy of pretty girls and the funny man outbid Mozart, out goes Mozart.

UNSER SHAKESPEAR

Before the war an effort was made to remedy this by establishing a national theatre in celebration of the tercentenary of the death of Shakespear. A committee was formed; and all sorts of illustrious and influential persons lent their names to a grand appeal to our national culture. My play, The Dark Lady of The Sonnets, was one of the incidents of that appeal. After some years of effort the result was a single handsome subscription from a German gentleman. Like the celebrated swearer in the anecdote when the cart containing all his household goods lost its tailboard at the top of the hill and let its contents roll in ruin to the bottom, I can only say, 'I cannot do justice to this situation,' and let it pass without another word.

THE HIGHER DRAMA PUT OUT OF ACTION

The effect of the war on the London theatres may now be imagined. The beds and the bevies drove every higher form of art out of it. Rents went up to an unprecedented figure. At the same time prices doubled everywhere except at the theatre payboxes, and raised the expenses of management to such a degree that unless the houses were quite full every night, profit was impossible. Even bare solvency could not be attained without a very wide popularity. Now what had made serious drama possible to a limited extent before the war was that a play could pay its way even if the theatre were only half full until Saturday and three-quarters full then. A manager who was an enthusiast and a desperately hard worker, with an occasional grant-in-aid from an artistically disposed millionaire, and a due proportion of those rare and happy accidents by which plays of the higher sort turn out to be potboilers as well, could hold out for some years, by which time a relay might arrive in the person of another enthusiast. Thus and not otherwise occurred that remarkable revival of the British drama at the beginning of the century which made my own career as a playwright possible in England. In America I had already established myself, not as part of the ordinary theatre system, but in association with the exceptional genius of Richard Mansfield. In Germany and Austria I had no difficulty: the system of publicly aided theatres there, Court and Municipal, kept drama of the kind I dealt in alive; so that I was indebted to the Emperor of Austria for magnificent productions of my works at a time when the sole official attention paid me by the British Court was the announcement to the English-speaking world that certain plays of mine were unfit for public performance, a substantial set-off against this being that the British Court, in the course of its private playgoing, paid no regard to the bad character given me by the chief officer of its household.

Howbeit, the fact that my plays effected a lodgment on the London stage, and were presently followed by the plays of Granville Barker, Gilbert Murray, John Masefield, St John Hankin, Laurence Housman, Arnold Bennett, John Galsworthy, John Drinkwater, and others which would in the nineteenth century have stood rather less chance of production at a London theatre than the Dialogues of Plato, not to mention revivals of the ancient Athenian drama, and a restoration to the stage of Shakespear's plays as he wrote them, was made economically possible solely by a supply of theatres which could hold nearly twice as much money as it cost to rent and maintain them. In such theatres work appealing to a relatively small class of cultivated persons, and therefore attracting only from half to three-quarters as many spectators as the more popular pastimes, could nevertheless keep going in the hands of young adventurers who were doing it for its own sake, and had not yet been forced by advancing age and responsibilities to consider the commercial value of their time and energy too closely. The war struck this foundation away in the manner I have just described. The expenses of running the cheapest west-end theatres rose to a sum which exceeded by twenty-five per cent the utmost that the higher drama can, as an ascertained matter of fact, be depended on to draw. Thus the higher drama, which has never really been a commercially sound speculation, now became an impossible one. Accordingly, attempts are being made to provide a refuge for it in suburban theatres in London and repertory theatres in the provinces. But at the moment when the army has at last disgorged the survivors of the gallant band of dramatic pioneers whom it swallowed, they find that the economic conditions which formerly made their work no worse than precarious now put it out of the question altogether, as far as the west end of London is concerned.

CHURCH AND THEATRE

I do not suppose many people care particularly. We are not brought up to care; and a sense of the national importance of the theatre is not born in mankind: the natural man, like so many of the soldiers at the beginning of the war, does not know what a theatre is. But please note that all these soldiers who did not know what a theatre was, knew what a church was. And they had been taught to respect churches. Nobody had ever warned them against a church as a place where frivolous women paraded in their best clothes; where stories of improper females like Potiphar's wife, and erotic poetry like the Song of Songs, were read aloud; where the sensuous and sentimental music of Schubert, Mendelssohn, Gounod, and Brahms was more popular than severe music by greater composers; where the prettiest sort of pretty pictures of pretty saints assailed the imagination and senses through stained-glass windows; and where sculpture and architecture came to the help of painting. Nobody ever reminded them that these things had sometimes produced such developments of erotic idolatry that men who were not only enthusiastic amateurs of literature, painting, and music, but famous practitioners of them, had actually exulted when mobs and even regular troops under express command had mutilated church statues, smashed church windows, wrecked church organs, and torn up the sheets from which the church music was read and sung. When they saw broken statues in churches, they were told that this was the work of wicked godless rioters, instead of, as it was, the work partly of zealots bent on driving the world, the flesh, and the devil out of the temple, and partly of insurgent men who had become intolerably poor because the temple had become a den of thieves. But all the sins and perversions that were so carefully hidden from them in the history of the Church were laid on the shoulders of the Theatre: that stuffy, uncomfortable place of penance in which we suffer so much inconvenience on the slenderest chance of gaining a scrap of food for our starving souls. When the Germans bombed the Cathedral of Rheims the world rang with the horror of the sacrilege. When they bombed the Little Theatre in the Adelphi, and narrowly missed bombing two writers of plays who lived within a few yards of it, the fact was not even mentioned in the papers. In point of appeal to the senses no theatre ever built could touch the fane at Rheims: no actress could rival its Virgin in beauty, nor any operatic tenor look otherwise than a fool beside its David. Its picture glass was glorious even to those who had seen the glass of Chartres. It was wonderful in its very grotesques: who would look at the Blondin Donkey after seeing its leviathans? In spite of the Adam-Adelphian decoration on which Miss Kingston had lavished so much taste and care, the Little Theatre was in comparison with Rheims the gloomiest of little conventicles: indeed the cathedral must, from the Puritan point of view, have debauched a million voluptuaries for every one whom the Little Theatre had sent home thoughtful to a chaste bed after Mr Chesterton's Magic or Brieux's *Les Avariés*. Perhaps that is the real reason why the Church is lauded and the Theatre reviled. Whether or no, the fact remains that the lady to whose public spirit and sense of the national value of the theatre I owed the first regular public performance of a play of mine had to conceal her action as if it had been a crime, whereas if she had given the money to the Church she would have worn a halo for it. And I admit, as I have always done, that this state of things may have been a very sensible one. I have asked Londoners again and again why they pay half a guinea to go to a theatre when they can go to St Paul's or Westminster Abbey for nothing. Their only possible reply is that they want to see something new and possibly something wicked; but the theatres mostly disappoint both hopes. If ever a revolution makes me Dictator, I shall establish a heavy charge for admission to our churches. But everyone who pays at the church door shall receive a ticket entitling him or her to free admission to one performance at any theatre he or she prefers. Thus shall the sensuous charms of the church service be made to subsidize the sterner virtue of the drama.

THE NEXT PHASE

The present situation will not last. Although the newspaper I read at breakfast this morning before writing these words contains a calculation that no less than twenty-three wars are at present being waged to confirm the peace, England is no longer in khaki; and a violent reaction is setting in against the crude theatrical fare of the four terrible years. Soon the rents of theatres will once more be fixed on the assumption that they cannot always be full, nor even on the average half full week in and week out. Prices will change. The higher drama will be at no greater disadvantage than it was before the war; and it may benefit, first, by the fact that many of us have been torn from the fools' paradise in which the theatre formerly traded, and thrust upon the sternest realities and necessities until we have lost both faith in and patience with the theatrical pretences that had no root either in reality or necessity; second, by the startling change made by the war in the distribution of income. It seems only the other day that a millionaire was a man with £50,000 a year. To-day, when he has paid his income tax and super tax, and insured his life for the amount of his death duties, he is lucky if his net income is £10,000, though his nominal property remains the same. And this is the result of a Budget which is called 'a respite for the rich.' At the other end of the scale millions of persons have had regular incomes for the first time in their lives; and their men have been regularly clothed, fed, lodged, and taught to make up their minds that certain things have to be done, also for the first time in their lives. Hundreds of thousands of women have been taken out of their domestic cages and tasted both discipline and independence. The thoughtless and snobbish middle classes have been pulled up short by the very unpleasant experience of being ruined to an unprecedented extent. We have all had a tremendous jolt; and although the widespread notion that the shock of the war would automatically make a new heaven and a new earth, and that the dog would never go back to his vomit nor the sow to her wallowing in the mire, is already seen to be a delusion, yet we are far more conscious of our condition than we were, and far less disposed to submit to it. Revolution, lately only a sensational chapter in history or a demagogic claptrap, is now a possibility so imminent that hardly by trying to suppress it in other countries by arms and defamation, and calling the process anti-Bolshevism, can our Government stave it off at home.

Perhaps the most tragic figure of the day is the American President who was once a historian. In those days it became his task to tell us how, after that great war in America which was more clearly than any other war of our time a war for an idea, the conquerors, confronted with a heroic task of reconstruction, turned recreant, and spent fifteen years in abusing their victory under cover of pretending to accomplish the task they were doing what they could to make impossible. Alas! Hegel was right when he said that we learn from history that men never learn anything from history. With what anguish of mind the President sees that we, the new conquerors, forgetting everything we professed to fight for, are sitting down with watering mouths to a good square meal of ten years revenge upon and humiliation of our prostrate foe, can only be guessed by those who know, as he does, how hopeless is remonstrance, and how happy Lincoln was in perishing from the earth before his inspired messages became scraps of paper. He knows well that from the

Peace Conference will come, in spite of his utmost, no edict on which he will be able, like Lincoln, to invoke 'the considerate judgment of mankind, and the gracious favor of Almighty God.' He led his people to destroy the militarism of Zabern; and the army they rescued is busy in Cologne imprisoning every German who does not salute a British officer; whilst the Government at home, asked whether it approves, replies that it does not propose even to discontinue this Zabernism when the Peace is concluded, but in effect looks forward to making Germans salute British officers until the end of the world. That is what war makes of men and women. It will wear off; and the worst it threatens is already proving impracticable; but before the humble and contrite heart ceases to be despised, the President and I, being of the same age, will be dotards. In the meantime there is, for him, another history to write; for me, another comedy to stage. Perhaps, after all, that is what wars are for, and what historians and playwrights are for. If men will not learn until their lessons are written in blood, why, blood they must have, their own for preference.

THE EPHEMERAL THRONES AND THE ETERNAL THEATRE

To the theatre it will not matter. Whatever Bastilles fall, the theatre will stand. Apostolic Hapsburg has collapsed; All Highest Hohenzollern languishes in Holland, threatened with trial on a capital charge of fighting for his country against England; Imperial Romanoff, said to have perished miserably by a more summary method of murder, is perhaps alive or perhaps dead: nobody cares more than if he had been a peasant; the lord of Hellas is level with his lackeys in republican Switzerland; Prime Ministers and Commanders-in-Chief have passed from a brief glory as Solons and Caesars into failure and obscurity as closely on one another's heels as the descendants of Banquo; but Euripides and

Aristophanes, Shakespear and Molière, Goethe and Ibsen remain fixed in their everlasting seats.

HOW WAR MUZZLES THE DRAMATIC POET

As for myself, why, it may be asked, did I not write two plays about the war instead of two pamphlets on it? The answer is significant. You cannot make war on war and on your neighbor at the same time. War cannot bear the terrible castigation of comedy, the ruthless light of laughter that glares on the stage. When men are heroically dying for their country, it is not the time to shew their lovers and wives and fathers and mothers how they are being sacrificed to the blunders of boobies, the cupidity of capitalists, the ambition of conquerors, the electioneering of demagogues, the Pharisaism of patriots, the lusts and lies and rancors and bloodthirsts that love war because it opens their prison doors, and sets them in the thrones of power and popularity. For unless these things are mercilessly exposed they will hide under the mantle of the ideals on the stage just as they do in real life.

And though there may be better things to reveal, it may not, and indeed cannot, be militarily expedient to reveal them whilst the issue is still in the balance. Truth telling is not compatible with the defence of the realm. We are just now reading the revelations of our generals and admirals, unmuzzled at last by the armistice. During the war, General A, in his moving despatches from the field, told how General B had covered himself with deathless glory in such and such a battle. He now tells us that General B came within an ace of losing us the war by disobeying his orders on that occasion, and fighting instead of running away as he ought to have done. An excellent subject for comedy now that the war is over, no doubt; but if General A had let this out at the time, what would have been the effect on General B's soldiers? And had the stage made known what the Prime Minister and the Secretary of State for War who overruled General A thought of him, and what he thought of them, as now revealed in raging controversy, what would have been the effect on the nation? That is why comedy, though sorely tempted, had to be loyally silent; for the art of the dramatic poet knows no patriotism; recognizes no obligation but truth to natural history; cares not whether Germany or England perish; is ready to cry with Brynhild, '*Lass' uns verderben, lachend zu Grunde geh'n*' sooner than deceive or be deceived; and thus becomes in time of war a greater military danger than poison, steel, or trinitrotoluene. That is why I had to withhold Heartbreak House from the footlights during the war; for the Germans might on any night have turned the last act from play into earnest, and even then might not have waited for their cues.

June 1919

ACT 1

The hilly country in the middle of the north edge of Sussex, looking very pleasant on a fine evening at the end of September, is seen through the windows of a room which has been built so as to resemble the after part of an old-fashioned high-pooped ship with a stern gallery; for the windows are ship built with heavy timbering, and run right across the room as continuously as the stability of the wall allows. A row of lockers under the windows provides an unupholstered window-seat interrupted by twin glass doors, respectively halfway between the stern post and the sides. Another door strains the illusion a little by being apparently in the ship's port side, and yet leading, not to the open sea, but to the entrance hall of the house. Between this door and the stern gallery are bookshelves. There are electric light switches beside the door leading to the hall and the glass doors in the stern gallery. Against the starboard wall is a carpenter's bench. The vice has a board in its jaws; and the floor is littered with shavings, overflowing from a waste-paper basket. A couple of planes and a centrebit are on the bench. In the same wall, between the bench and the windows, is a narrow doorway with a half door, above which a glimpse of the room beyond shews that it is a shelved pantry with bottles and kitchen crockery.

On the starboard side, but close to the middle, is a plain oak drawing-table with drawing-board, T-square, straightedges, set squares, mathematical instruments, saucers of water color, a tumbler of discolored water, Indian ink, pencils, and brushes on it. The drawing-board is set so that the draughtsman's chair has the window on its left hand. On the floor at the end of the table, on his right, is a ship's fire bucket. On the port side of the room, near the bookshelves, is a sofa with its back to the windows. It is a sturdy mahogany article, oddly upholstered in sailcloth, including the bolster, with a couple of blankets hanging over the back. Between the sofa and the drawing-table is a big wicker chair, with broad arms and a low sloping back, with its back to the light. A small but stout table of teak, with a round top and gate legs, stands against the port wall between the door and the bookcase. It is the only article in the room that suggests (not at all convincingly) a woman's hand in the furnishing. The uncarpeted floor of narrow boards is caulked and holystoned like a deck.

The garden to which the glass doors lead dips to the south before the landscape rises again to the hills. Emerging from the hollow is the cupola of an observatory. Between the observatory and the house is a flagstaff on a little esplanade, with a hammock on the east side and a long garden seat on the west.

A young lady, gloved and hatted, with a dust coat on, is sitting in the window-seat with her body twisted to enable her to look out at the view. One hand props her chin: the other hangs down with a volume of the Temple Shakespear in it, and her finger stuck in the page she has been reading.

A clock strikes six.

The young lady turns and looks at her watch. She rises with an air of one who waits and is almost at the end of her patience. She is a pretty girl, slender, fair, and intelligent looking, nicely but not expensively dressed, evidently not a smart idler.

With a sigh of weary resignation she comes to the draughtsman's chair; sits down; and begins to read Shakespear. Presently the book sinks to her lap; her eyes close; and she dozes into a slumber.

An elderly womanservant comes in from the hall with three unopened bottles of rum on a tray. She passes through and disappears in the pantry without noticing the young lady. She places the bottles on the shelf and fills her tray with empty bottles. As she returns with these, the young lady lets her book drop, awakening herself, and startling the womanservant so that she all but lets the tray fall.

THE WOMANSERVANT. God bless us! [*The young lady picks up the book and places it on the table*]. Sorry to wake you, miss, I'm sure; but you are a stranger to me. What might you be waiting here for now?

THE YOUNG LADY. Waiting for somebody to shew some signs of knowing that I have been invited here.

THE WOMANSERVANT. Oh, youre invited, are you? And has nobody come? Dear! dear!

THE YOUNG LADY. A wild-looking old gentleman came and looked in at the window; and I heard him calling out 'Nurse: there is a young and attractive female waiting in the poop. Go and see what she wants.' Are you the nurse?

THE WOMANSERVANT. Yes, miss: I'm Nurse Guinness. That was old Captain Shotover, Mrs Hushabye's father. I heard him roaring; but I thought it was for something else. I suppose it was Mrs Hushabye that invited you, ducky?

THE YOUNG LADY. I understood her to do so. But really I think I'd better go.

NURSE GUINNESS. Oh, dont think of such a thing, miss. If Mrs Hushabye has forgotten all about it, it will be a pleasant surprise for her to see you, wont it?

THE YOUNG LADY. It has been a very unpleasant surprise to me to find that nobody expects me.

NURSE GUINNESS. Youll get used to it, miss: this house is full of surprises for them that dont know our ways.

CAPTAIN SHOTOVER [*looking in from the hall suddenly: an ancient but still hardy man with an immense white beard, in a reefer jacket with a whistle hanging from his neck*] Nurse: there is a hold-all and a handbag on the front steps for everybody to fall over. Also a tennis racquet. Who the devil left them there?

THE YOUNG LADY. They are mine, I'm afraid.

THE CAPTAIN [*advancing to the drawing-table*] Nurse: who is this misguided and unfortunate young lady?

NURSE GUINNESS. She says Miss Hessy invited her, sir.

THE CAPTAIN. And had she no friend, no parents, to warn her against my daughter's invitations? This is a pretty sort of house, by heavens! A young and attractive lady is invited here. Her luggage is left on the steps for hours; and she herself is deposited in the poop and abandoned, tired and starving. This is our hospitality. These are our manners. No room ready. No hot water. No welcoming hostess. Our visitor is to sleep in the toolshed, and to wash in the duckpond.

NURSE GUINNESS. Now it's all right, Captain: I'll get the lady some tea; and her room shall be ready before she has finished it. [*To the young lady*] Take off your hat, ducky; and make yourself at home [*she goes to the door leading to the hall*].

THE CAPTAIN [*as she passes him*] Ducky! Do you suppose, woman, that because this young lady has been insulted and neglected, you have the right to address her as you address my wretched children, whom you have brought up in ignorance of the commonest decencies of social intercourse?

NURSE GUINNESS. Never mind him, doty. [*Quite unconcerned, she goes out into the hall on her way to the kitchen*].

THE CAPTAIN. Madam: will you favor me with your name? [*He sits down in the big wicker chair*].

THE YOUNG LADY. My name is Ellie Dunn.

THE CAPTAIN. Dunn! I had a boatswain whose name was Dunn. He was originally a pirate in China. He set up as a ship's chandler with stores which I have every reason to believe he stole from me. No doubt he became rich. Are you his daughter?

ELLIE [*indignant*] No: certainly not. I am proud to be able to say that though my father has not been a successful man, nobody has ever had one word to say against him. I think my father is the best man I have ever known.

THE CAPTAIN. He must be greatly changed. Has he attained the seventh degree of concentration?

ELLIE. I dont understand.

THE CAPTAIN. But how could he, with a daughter! I, madam, have two daughters. One of them is Hesione Husha-

bye, who invited you here. I keep this house: she upsets it.
I desire to attain the seventh degree of concentration: she
invites visitors and leaves me to entertain them. [*Nurse
Guinness returns with the tea-tray, which she places on the teak
table*]. I have a second daughter who is, thank God, in a
remote part of the Empire with her numskull of a husband.
As a child she thought the figure-head of my ship, the
Dauntless, the most beautiful thing on earth. He re-
sembled it. He had the same expression: wooden yet enterprising. She married him, and will never set foot in this
house again.

NURSE GUINNESS [*carrying the table, with the tea-things on it, to
Ellie's side*] Indeed you never were more mistaken. She is
in England this very moment. You have been told three
times this week that she is coming home for a year for her
health. And very glad you should be to see your own
daughter again after all these years.

THE CAPTAIN. I am not glad. The natural term of the
affection of the human animal for its offspring is six years.
My daughter Ariadne was born when I was forty-six. I
am now eighty-eight. If she comes, I am not at home. If
she wants anything, let her take it. If she asks for me, let
her be informed that I am extremely old, and have totally
forgotten her.

NURSE GUINNESS. Thats no talk to offer to a young lady.
Here, ducky, have some tea; and dont listen to him [*she
pours out a cup of tea*].

THE CAPTAIN [*rising wrathfully*] Now before high heaven
they have given this innocent child Indian tea: the stuff
they tan their own leather insides with. [*He seizes the cup
and the tea-pot and empties both into the leathern bucket*].

ELLIE [*almost in tears*] Oh, please! I am so tired. I should
have been glad of anything.

NURSE GUINNESS. Oh, what a thing to do! The poor lamb is
ready to drop.

THE CAPTAIN. You shall have some of my tea. Do not touch that fly-blown cake: nobody eats it here except the dogs. [*He disappears into the pantry*].

NURSE GUINNESS. Theres a man for you! They say he sold himself to the devil in Zanzibar before he was a captain; and the older he grows the more I believe them.

A WOMAN'S VOICE [*in the hall*] Is anyone at home? Hesione! Nurse! Papa! Do come, somebody; and take in my luggage.

Thumping heard, as of an umbrella, on the wainscot.

NURSE GUINNESS. My gracious! It's Miss Addie, Lady Utterword, Mrs Hushabye's sister: the one I told the Captain about. [*Calling*] Coming, Miss, coming.

She carries the table back to its place by the door, and is hurrying out when she is intercepted by Lady Utterword, who bursts in much flustered. Lady Utterword, a blonde, is very handsome, very well dressed, and so precipitate in speech and action that the first impression (erroneous) is one of comic silliness.

LADY UTTERWORD. Oh, is that you, Nurse? How are you? You dont look a day older. Is nobody at home? Where is Hesione? Doesnt she expect me? Where are the servants? Whose luggage is that on the steps? Where's Papa? Is everybody asleep? [*Seeing Ellie*] Oh! I beg your pardon. I suppose you are one of my nieces. [*Approaching her with outstretched arms*] Come and kiss your aunt, darling.

ELLIE. I'm only a visitor. It is my luggage on the steps.

NURSE GUINNESS. I'll go get you some fresh tea, ducky. [*She takes up the tray*].

ELLIE. But the old gentleman said he would make some himself.

NURSE GUINNESS. Bless you! he's forgotten what he went for already. His mind wanders from one thing to another.

LADY UTTERWORD. Papa, I suppose?

NURSE GUINNESS. Yes, Miss.

LADY UTTERWORD [*vehemently*] Dont be silly, nurse. Dont call me Miss.

NURSE GUINNESS [*placidly*] No, lovey [*she goes out with the tea-tray*].

LADY UTTERWORD [*sitting down with a flounce on the sofa*] I know what you must feel. Oh, this house, this house! I come back to it after twenty-three years; and it is just the same: the luggage lying on the steps, the servants spoilt and impossible, nobody at home to receive anybody, no regular meals, nobody ever hungry because they are always gnawing bread and butter or munching apples, and, what is worse, the same disorder in ideas, in talk, in feeling. When I was a child I was used to it: I had never known anything better, though I was unhappy, and longed all the time – oh, how I longed! – to be respectable, to be a lady, to live as others did, not to have to think of everything for myself. I married at nineteen to escape from it. My husband is Sir Hastings Utterword, who has been governor of all the crown colonies in succession. I have always been the mistress of Government House. I have been so happy: I had forgotten that people could live like this. I wanted to see my father, my sister, my nephews and nieces (one ought to, you know), and I was looking forward to it. And now the state of the house! the way I'm received! the casual impudence of that woman Guinness, our old nurse! really Hesione might at least have been here: some preparation might have been made for me. You must excuse my going on in this way; but I am really very much hurt and annoyed and disillusioned: and if I had realized it was to be like this, I wouldnt have come. I have a great mind to go away without another word [*she is on the point of weeping*].

ELLIE [*also very miserable*] Nobody has been here to receive me either. I thought I ought to go away too. But how can I, Lady Utterword? My luggage is on the steps; and the station fly has gone.

The Captain emerges from the pantry with a tray of Chinese lacquer and a very fine tea-set on it. He rests it provisionally on the end of the table; snatches away the drawing-board, which he stands on the floor against the table legs; and puts the tray in the space thus cleared. Ellie pours out a cup greedily.

THE CAPTAIN. Your tea, young lady. What! another lady! I must fetch another cup [*he makes for the pantry*].

LADY UTTERWORD [*rising from the sofa, suffused with emotion*] Papa! Dont you know me? I'm your daughter.

THE CAPTAIN. Nonsense! my daughter's upstairs asleep. [*He vanishes through the half door*].

Lady Utterword retires to the window to conceal her tears.

ELLIE [*going to her with the cup*] Dont be so distressed. Have this cup of tea. He is very old and very strange: he has been just like that to me. I know how dreadful it must be: my own father is all the world to me. Oh, I'm sure he didnt mean it.

The Captain returns with another cup.

THE CAPTAIN. Now we are complete. [*He places it on the tray*].

LADY UTTERWORD [*hysterically*] Papa: you cant have forgotten me. I am Ariadne. I'm little Paddy Patkins. Wont you kiss me? [*She goes to him and throws her arms round his neck*].

THE CAPTAIN [*woodenly enduring her embrace*] How can you be Ariadne? You are a middle-aged woman: well preserved, madam, but no longer young.

LADY UTTERWORD. But think of all the years and years I have been away, Papa. I have had to grow old, like other people.

THE CAPTAIN [*disengaging himself*] You should grow out of kissing strange men: they may be striving to attain the seventh degree of concentration.

LADY UTTERWORD. But I'm your daughter. You havnt seen me for years.

THE CAPTAIN. So much the worse! When our relatives are at home, we have to think of all their good points or it would be impossible to endure them. But when they are away, we console ourselves for their absence by dwelling on their vices. That is how I have come to think my absent daughter Ariadne a perfect fiend; so do not try to ingratiate yourself here by impersonating her [*he walks firmly away to the other side of the room*].

LADY UTTERWORD. Ingratiating myself indeed! [*With dignity*] Very well, papa. [*She sits down at the drawing-table and pours out tea for herself*].

THE CAPTAIN. I am neglecting my social duties. You remember Dunn? Billy Dunn?

LADY UTTERWORD. Do you mean that villainous sailor who robbed you?

THE CAPTAIN [*introducing Ellie*] His daughter. [*He sits down on the sofa*].

ELLIE [*protesting*] No –

Nurse Guinness returns with fresh tea.

THE CAPTAIN. Take that hogwash away. Do you hear?

NURSE. Youve actually remembered about the tea! [*To Ellie*] O, miss, he didnt forget you after all! You have made an impression.

THE CAPTAIN [*gloomily*] Youth! beauty! novelty! They are badly wanted in this house. I am excessively old. Hesione is only moderately young. Her children are not youthful.

LADY UTTERWORD. How can children be expected to be youthful in this house? Almost before we could speak we were filled with notions that might have been all very well for pagan philosophers of fifty, but were certainly quite unfit for respectable people of any age.

NURSE. You were always for respectability, Miss Addy.

LADY UTTERWORD. Nurse: will you please remember that I am Lady Utterword, and not Miss Addy, nor lovey, nor darling, nor doty? Do you hear?

NURSE. Yes, ducky: all right, I'll tell them all they must call you my lady. [*She takes her tray out with undisturbed placidity*].

LADY UTTERWORD. What comfort? what sense is there in having servants with no manners?

ELLIE [*rising and coming to the table to put down her empty cup*] Lady Utterword: do you think Mrs Hushabye really expects me?

LADY UTTERWORD. Oh, dont ask me. You can see for yourself that Ive just arrived; her only sister, after twenty-three years absence! and it seems that *I* am not expected.

THE CAPTAIN. What does it matter whether the young lady is expected or not? She is welcome. There are beds: there is food. I'll find a room for her myself [*he makes for the door*].

ELLIE [*following him to stop him*] Oh please – [*he goes out*]. Lady Utterword: I dont know what to do. Your father persists in believing that my father is some sailor who robbed him.

LADY UTTERWORD. You had better pretend not to notice it. My father is a very clever man; but he always forgot things; and now that he is old, of course he is worse. And I must warn you that it is sometimes very hard to feel quite sure that he really forgets.

Mrs Hushabye bursts into the room tempestuously, and embraces Ellie. She is a couple of years older than Lady Utterword and even better looking. She has magnificent black hair, eyes like the fishpools of Heshbon, and a nobly modelled neck, short at the back and low between her shoulders in front. Unlike her sister she is uncorseted and dressed anyhow in a rich robe of black pile that shews off her white skin and statuesque contour.

MRS HUSHABYE. Ellie, my darling, my pettikins [*kissing her*]: how long have you been here? Ive been at home all the time: I was putting flowers and things in your room; and when I just sat down for a moment to try how comfortable the armchair was I went off to sleep. Papa woke me and told me you were here. Fancy you finding no one, and being neglected and abandoned. [*Kissing her again*]. My poor love! [*She deposits Ellie on the sofa. Meanwhile*

Ariadne has left the table and come over to claim her share of attention]. Oh! youve brought someone with you. Introduce me.

LADY UTTERWORD. Hesione: is it possible that you dont know me?

MRS HUSHABYE [*conventionally*] Of course I remember your face quite well. Where have we met?

LADY UTTERWORD. Didnt Papa tell you I was here? Oh! this is really too much. [*She throws herself sulkily into the big chair*].

MRS HUSHABYE. Papa!

LADY UTTERWORD. Yes: Papa. Our papa, you unfeeling wretch. [*Rising angrily*] I'll go straight to a hotel.

MRS HUSHABYE [*seizing her by the shoulders*] My goodness gracious goodness, you dont mean to say that youre Addy!

LADY UTTERWORD. I certainly am Addy; and I dont think I can be so changed that you would not have recognized me if you had any real affection for me. And Papa didnt think me even worth mentioning!

MRS HUSHABYE. What a lark! Sit down [*she pushes her back into the chair instead of kissing her, and posts herself behind it*]. You do look a swell. Youre much handsomer than you used to be. Youve made the acquaintance of Ellie of course. She is going to marry a perfect hog of a millionaire for the sake of her father, who is as poor as a church mouse; and you must help me to stop her.

ELLIE. Oh please, Hesione.

MRS HUSHABYE. My pettikins, the man's coming here today with your father to begin persecuting you; and everybody will see the state of the case in ten minutes; so whats the use of making a secret of it?

ELLIE. He is not a hog, Hesione. You dont know how wonderfully good he was to my father, and how deeply grateful I am to him.

MRS HUSHABYE [*to Lady Utterword*] Her father is a very

remarkable man, Addy. His name is Mazzini Dunn. Mazzini was a celebrity of some kind who knew Ellie's grandparents. They were both poets, like the Brownings; and when her father came into the world Mazzini said 'Another soldier born for freedom!' So they christened him Mazzini; and he has been fighting for freedom in his quiet way ever since. Thats why he is so poor.

ELLIE. I am proud of his poverty.

MRS HUSHABYE. Of course you are, pettikins. Why not leave him in it, and marry someone you love?

LADY UTTERWORD [*rising suddenly and explosively*] Hesione: are you going to kiss me or are you not?

MRS HUSHABYE. What do you want to be kissed for?

LADY UTTERWORD. I dont want to be kissed; but I do want you to behave properly and decently. We are sisters. We have been separated for twenty-three years. You ought to kiss me.

MRS HUSHABYE. Tomorrow morning, dear, before you make up. I hate the smell of powder.

LADY UTTERWORD. Oh! you unfeeling – [*she is interrupted by the return of the captain*].

THE CAPTAIN [*to Ellie*] Your room is ready. [*Ellie rises*]. The sheets were damp; but I have changed them [*he makes for the garden door on the port side*].

LADY UTTERWORD. Oh! What about my sheets?

THE CAPTAIN [*halting at the door*] Take my advice: air them; or take them off and sleep in blankets. You shall sleep in Ariadne's old room.

LADY UTTERWORD. Indeed I shall do nothing of the sort. That little hole! I am entitled to the best spare room.

THE CAPTAIN [*continuing unmoved*] She married a numskull. She told me she would marry anyone to get away from home.

LADY UTTERWORD. You are pretending not to know me on purpose. I will leave the house.

Mazzini Dunn enters from the hall. He is a little elderly man with bulging credulous eyes and an earnest manner. He is dressed in a blue serge jacket suit with an unbuttoned mackintosh over it, and carries a soft black hat of clerical cut.

ELLIE. At last! Captain Shotover: here is my father.

THE CAPTAIN. This! Nonsense! not a bit like him [*he goes away through the garden, shutting the door sharply behind him*].

LADY UTTERWORD. I will not be ignored and pretended to be somebody else. I will have it out with papa now, this instant. [*To Mazzini*] Excuse me. [*She follows the Captain out, making a hasty bow to Mazzini, who returns it*].

MRS HUSHABYE [*hospitably, shaking hands*] How good of you to come, Mr Dunn! You dont mind papa, do you? He is as mad as a hatter, you know, but quite harmless, and extremely clever. You will have some delightful talks with him.

MAZZINI. I hope so. [*To Ellie*] So here you are, Ellie dear. [*He draws her arm affectionately through his*]. I must thank you, Mrs Hushabye, for your kindness to my daughter. I'm afraid she would have had no holiday if you had not invited her.

MRS HUSHABYE. Not at all. Very nice of her to come and attract young people to the house for us.

MAZZINI [*smiling*] I'm afraid Ellie is not interested in young men, Mrs Hushabye. Her taste is on the graver, solider side.

MRS HUSHABYE [*with a sudden rather hard brightness in her manner*] Wont you take off your overcoat, Mr Dunn? You will find a cupboard for coats and hats and things in the corner of the hall.

MAZZINI [*hastily releasing Ellie*] Yes – thank you – I had better – [*he goes out*].

MRS HUSHABYE [*emphatically*] The old brute!

ELLIE. Who?

MRS HUSHABYE. Who! Him. He. It [*pointing after Mazzini*]. 'Graver, solider tastes,' indeed!

ELLIE [*aghast*] You dont mean that you were speaking like that of my father!

MRS HUSHABYE. I was. You know I was.

ELLIE [*with dignity*] I will leave your house at once. [*She turns to the door*].

MRS HUSHABYE. If you attempt it, I'll tell your father why.

ELLIE [*turning again*] Oh! How can you treat a visitor like this, Mrs Hushabye?

MRS HUSHABYE. I thought you were going to call me Hesione.

ELLIE. Certainly not now!

MRS HUSHABYE. Very well: I'll tell your father.

ELLIE [*distressed*] Oh!

MRS HUSHABYE. If you turn a hair – if you take his part against me and against your own heart for a moment, I'll give that born soldier of freedom a piece of my mind that will stand him on his selfish old head for a week.

ELLIE. Hesione! My father selfish! How little you know –

    She is interrupted by Mazzini, who returns, excited and perspiring.

MAZZINI. Ellie: Mangan has come: I thought youd like to know. Excuse me, Mrs Hushabye: the strange old gentleman –

MRS HUSHABYE. Papa. Quite so.

MAZZINI. Oh, I beg your pardon: of course: I was a little confused by his manner. He is making Mangan help him with something in the garden; and he wants me too –

    A powerful whistle is heard.

THE CAPTAIN'S VOICE. Bosun ahoy! [*the whistle is repeated*].

MAZZINI [*flustered*] Oh dear! I believe he is whistling for me. [*He hurries out*].

MRS HUSHABYE. Now my father is a wonderful man if you like.

ELLIE. Hesione: listen to me. You dont understand. My father and Mr Mangan were boys together. Mr Ma—

MRS HUSHABYE. I dont care what they were: we must sit down if you are going to begin as far back as that [*She snatches at Ellie's waist, and makes her sit down on the sofa beside her*]. Now, pettikins: tell me all about Mr Mangan. They call him Boss Mangan, dont they? He is a Napoleon of industry and disgustingly rich, isnt he? Why isnt your father rich?

ELLIE. My poor father should never have been in business. His parents were poets; and they gave him the noblest ideas; but they could not afford to give him a profession.

MRS HUSHABYE. Fancy your grandparents, with their eyes in fine frenzy rolling! And so your poor father had to go into business. Hasnt he succeeded in it?

ELLIE. He always used to say he could succeed if he only had some capital. He fought his way along, to keep a roof over our heads and bring us up well; but it was always a struggle: always the same difficulty of not having capital enough. I dont know how to describe it to you.

MRS HUSHABYE. Poor Ellie! I know. Pulling the devil by the tail.

ELLIE [*hurt*] Oh no. Not like that. It was at least dignified.

MRS HUSHABYE. That made it all the harder, didnt it? *I* shouldnt have pulled the devil by the tail with dignity. I should have pulled hard – [*between her teeth*] hard. Well? Go on.

ELLIE. At last it seemed that all our troubles were at an end. Mr Mangan did an extraordinarily noble thing out of pure friendship for my father and respect for his character. He asked him how much capital he wanted, and gave it to him. I dont mean that he lent it to him, or that he invested it in his business. He just simply made him a present of it. Wasnt that splendid of him?

MRS HUSHABYE. On condition that you married him?

ELLIE. Oh no, no, no. This was when I was a child. He had

never even seen me: he never came to our house. It was absolutely disinterested. Pure generosity.

MRS HUSHABYE. Oh! I beg the gentleman's pardon. Well, what became of the money?

ELLIE. We all got new clothes and moved into another house. And I went to another school for two years.

MRS HUSHABYE. Only two years?

ELLIE. That was all; for at the end of two years my father was utterly ruined.

MRS HUSHABYE. How?

ELLIE. I dont know. I never could understand. But it was dreadful. When we were poor my father had never been in debt. But when he launched out into business on a large scale, he had to incur liabilities. When the business went into liquidation he owed more money than Mr Mangan had given him.

MRS HUSHABYE. Bit off more than he could chew, I suppose.

ELLIE. I think you are a little unfeeling about it.

MRS HUSHABYE. My pettikins: you mustnt mind my way of talking. I was quite as sensitive and particular as you once; but I have picked up so much slang from the children that I am really hardly presentable. I suppose your father had no head for business, and made a mess of it.

ELLIE. Oh, that just shews how entirely you are mistaken about him. The business turned out a great success. It now pays forty-four per cent after deducting the excess profits tax.

MRS HUSHABYE. Then why arnt you rolling in money?

ELLIE. I dont know. It seems very unfair to me. You see, my father was made bankrupt. It nearly broke his heart, because he had persuaded several of his friends to put money into the business. He was sure it would succeed; and events proved that he was quite right. But they all lost their money. It was dreadful. I dont know what we should have done but for Mr Mangan.

MRS HUSHABYE. What! Did the Boss come to the rescue again, after all his money being thrown away?

ELLIE. He did indeed, and never uttered a reproach to my father. He bought what was left of the business – the buildings and the machinery and things – from the official trustee for enough money to enable my father to pay six and eightpence in the pound and get his discharge. Everyone pitied papa so much, and saw so plainly that he was an honorable man, that they let him off at six-and-eightpence instead of ten shillings. Then Mr Mangan started a company to take up the business, and made my father a manager in it to save us from starvation; for I wasnt earning anything then.

MRS HUSHABYE. Quite a romance. And when did the Boss develop the tender passion?

ELLIE. Oh, that was years after, quite lately. He took the chair one night at a sort of people's concert. I was singing there. As an amateur, you know: half a guinea for expenses and three songs with three encores. He was so pleased with my singing that he asked might he walk home with me. I never saw anyone so taken aback as he was when I took him home and introduced him to my father: his own manager. It was then that my father told me how nobly he had behaved. Of course it was considered a great chance for me, as he is so rich. And – and – we drifted into a sort of understanding – I suppose I should call it an engagement – [she is distressed and cannot go on].

MRS HUSHABYE [rising and marching about] You may have drifted into it; but you will bounce out of it, my pettikins, if I am to have anything to do with it.

ELLIE [hopelessly] No: it's no use. I am bound in honor and gratitude. I will go through with it.

MRS HUSHABYE [behind the sofa, scolding down at her] You know, of course, that it's not honorable or grateful to marry a man you dont love. Do you love this Mangan man?

ELLIE. Yes. At least –

MRS HUSHABYE. I dont want to know about 'the least': I want to know the worst. Girls of your age fall in love with all sorts of impossible people, especially old people.

ELLIE. I like Mr Mangan very much; and I shall always be –

MRS HUSHABYE [*impatiently completing the sentence and prancing away intolerantly to starboard*] – grateful to him for his kindness to dear father. I know. Anybody else?

ELLIE. What do you mean?

MRS HUSHABYE. Anybody else? Are you in love with anybody else?

ELLIE. Of course not.

MRS HUSHABYE. Humph! [*The book on the drawing-table catches her eye. She picks it up, and evidently finds the title very unexpected. She looks at Ellie, and asks, quaintly*]. Quite sure youre not in love with an actor?

ELLIE. No, no. Why? What put such a thing into your head?

MRS HUSHABYE. This is yours, isnt it? Why else should you be reading Othello?

ELLIE. My father taught me to love Shakespear.

MRS HUSHABYE [*flinging the book down on the table*] Really! your father does seem to be about the limit.

ELLIE [*naïvely*] Do you never read Shakespear, Hesione? That seems to me so extraordinary. I like Othello.

MRS HUSHABYE. Do you indeed? He was jealous, wasn't he?

ELLIE. Oh, not that. I think all the part about jealousy is horrible. But dont you think it must have been a wonderful experience for Desdemona, brought up so quietly at home, to meet a man who had been out in the world doing all sorts of brave things and having terrible adventures, and yet finding something in her that made him love to sit and talk with her and tell her about them?

MRS HUSHABYE. Thats your idea of romance, is it?

ELLIE. Not romance, exactly. It might really happen.

Ellie's eyes shew that she is not arguing, but in a daydream. Mrs Hushabye, watching her inquisitively, goes deliberately back to the sofa and resumes her seat beside her.

MRS HUSHABYE. Ellie darling: have you noticed that some of those stories that Othello told Desdemona couldnt have happened?

ELLIE. Oh no. Shakespear thought they could have happened.

MRS HUSHABYE. Hm! Desdemona thought they could have happened. But they didnt.

ELLIE. Why do you look so enigmatic about it? You are such a sphinx: I never know what you mean.

MRS HUSHABYE. Desdemona would have found him out if she had lived, you know. I wonder was that why he strangled her!

ELLIE. Othello was not telling lies.

MRS HUSHABYE. How do you know?

ELLIE. Shakespear would have said if he was. Hesione: there are men who have done wonderful things: men like Othello, only, of course, white, and very handsome, and –

MRS HUSHABYE. Ah! Now we're coming to it. Tell me all about him. I knew there must be somebody, or youd never have been so miserable about Mangan: youd have thought it quite a lark to marry him.

ELLIE [*blushing vividly*] Hesione: you are dreadful. But I dont want to make a secret of it, though of course I dont tell everybody. Besides, I dont know him.

MRS HUSHABYE. Dont know him! What does that mean?

ELLIE. Well, of course I know him to speak to.

MRS HUSHABYE. But you want to know him ever so much more intimately, eh?

ELLIE. No no: I know him quite – almost intimately.

MRS HUSHABYE. You dont know him; and you know him almost intimately. How lucid!

ELLIE. I mean that he does not call on us. I – I got into conversation with him by chance at a concert.

MRS HUSHABYE. You seem to have rather a gay time at your concerts, Ellie.

ELLIE. Not at all: we talk to everyone in the green-room waiting for our turns. I thought he was one of the artists: he looked so splendid. But he was only one of the committee. I happened to tell him that I was copying a picture at the National Gallery. I make a little money that way. I cant paint much; but as it's always the same picture I can do it pretty quickly and get two or three pounds for it. It happened that he came to the National Gallery one day.

MRS HUSHABYE. One student's day. Paid sixpence to stumble about through a crowd of easels, when he might have come in next day for nothing and found the floor clear! Quite by accident?

ELLIE [triumphantly] No. On purpose. He liked talking to me. He knows lots of the most splendid people. Fashionable women who are all in love with him. But he ran away from them to see me at the National Gallery and persuade me to come with him for a drive round Richmond Park in a taxi.

MRS HUSHABYE. My pettikins, you have been going it. It's wonderful what you good girls can do without anyone saying a word.

ELLIE. I am not in society, Hesione. If I didnt make acquaintances in that way I shouldnt have any at all.

MRS HUSHABYE. Well, no harm if you know how to take care of yourself. May I ask his name?

ELLIE [slowly and musically] Marcus Darnley.

MRS HUSHABYE [echoing the music] Marcus Darnley! What a splendid name!

ELLIE. Oh, I'm so glad you think so. I think so too; but I was afraid it was only a silly fancy of my own.

MRS HUSHABYE. Hm! Is he one of the Aberdeen Darnleys?

ELLIE. Nobody knows. Just fancy! He was found in an antique chest –

MRS HUSHABYE. A what?

ELLIE. An antique chest, one summer morning in a rose garden, after a night of the most terrible thunderstorm.

MRS HUSHABYE. What on earth was he doing in the chest? Did he get into it because he was afraid of the lightning?

ELLIE. Oh no, no: he was a baby. The name Marcus Darnley was embroidered on his babyclothes. And five hundred pounds in gold.

MRS HUSHABYE [*looking hard at her*] Ellie!

ELLIE. The garden of the Viscount –

MRS HUSHABYE. – de Rougemont?

ELLIE [*innocently*] No: de Larochejaquelin. A French family. A vicomte. His life has been one long romance. A tiger –

MRS HUSHABYE. Slain by his own hand?

ELLIE. Oh no: nothing vulgar like that. He saved the life of the tiger from a hunting party: one of King Edward's hunting parties in India. The King was furious: that was why he never had his military services properly recognized. But he doesnt care. He is a Socialist and despises rank, and has been in three revolutions fighting on the barricades.

MRS HUSHABYE. How can you sit there telling me such lies? You, Ellie, of all people! And I thought you were a perfectly simple, straightforward good girl.

ELLIE [*rising, dignified but very angry*] Do you mean to say you dont believe me?

MRS HUSHABYE. Of course I dont believe you. Youre inventing every word of it. Do you take me for a fool?

Ellie stares at her. Her candor is so obvious that Mrs Hushabye is puzzled.

ELLIE. Goodbye, Hesione. I'm very sorry. I see now that it

sounds very improbable as I tell it. But I cant stay if you think that way about me.

MRS HUSHABYE [*catching her dress*] You shant go. I couldnt be so mistaken: I know too well what liars are like. Somebody has really told you all this.

ELLIE [*flushing*] Hesione: dont say that you dont believe him. I couldnt bear that.

MRS HUSHABYE [*soothing her*] Of course I believe him, dearest. But you should have broken it to me by degrees. [*Drawing her back to the seat*] Now tell me all about him. Are you in love with him?

ELLIE. Oh no, I'm not so foolish. I dont fall in love with people. I'm not so silly as you think.

MRS HUSHABYE. I see. Only something to think about – to give some interest and pleasure to life.

ELLIE. Just so. Thats all, really.

MRS HUSHABYE. It makes the hours go fast, doesnt it? No tedious waiting to go to sleep at nights and wondering whether you will have a bad night. How delightful it makes waking up in the morning! How much better than the happiest dream! All life transfigured! No more wishing one had an interesting book to read, because life is so much happier than any book! No desire but to be alone and not to have to talk to anyone: to be alone and just think about it.

ELLIE [*embracing her*] Hesione: you are a witch. How do you know? Oh, you are the most sympathetic woman in the world.

MRS HUSHABYE [*caressing her*] Pettikins, my pettikins: how I envy you! and how I pity you!

ELLIE. Pity me! Oh, why?

A very handsome man of fifty, with mousquetaire moustaches, wearing a rather dandified curly brimmed hat, and carrying an elaborate walking-stick, comes into the room from the hall, and stops short at sight of the women on the sofa.

ELLIE [*seeing him and rising in glad surprise*] Oh! Hesione: this is Mr Marcus Darnley.

MRS HUSHABYE [*rising*] What a lark! He is my husband.

ELLIE. But how – [*she stops suddenly; then turns pale and sways*].

MRS HUSHABYE [*catching her and sitting down with her on the sofa*] Steady, my pettikins.

THE MAN [*with a mixture of confusion and effrontery, depositing his hat and stick on the teak table*] My real name, Miss Dunn, is Hector Hushabye. I leave you to judge whether that is a name any sensitive man would care to confess to. I never use it when I can possibly help it. I have been away for nearly a month; and I had no idea you knew my wife, or that you were coming here. I am none the less delighted to find you in our little house.

ELLIE [*in great distress*] I dont know what to do. Please, may I speak to papa? Do leave me. I cant bear it.

MRS HUSHABYE. Be off, Hector.

HECTOR. I –

MRS HUSHABYE. Quick, quick. Get out.

HECTOR. If you think it better – [*he goes out, taking his hat with him but leaving the stick on the table*].

MRS HUSHABYE [*laying Ellie down at the end of the sofa*] Now, pettikins, he is gone. Theres nobody but me. You can let yourself go. Dont try to control yourself. Have a good cry.

ELLIE [*raising her head*] Damn!

MRS HUSHABYE. Splendid! Oh, what a relief! I thought you were going to be broken-hearted. Never mind me. Damn him again.

ELLIE. I am not damning him: I am damning myself for being such a fool. [*Rising*] How could I let myself be taken in so? [*She begins prowling to and fro, her bloom gone, looking curiously older and harder*].

MRS HUSHABYE [*cheerfully*] Why not, pettikins? Very few young women can resist Hector. I couldnt when I was your age. He is really rather splendid, you know.

ELLIE [*turning on her*] Splendid! Yes: splendid looking, of course. But how can you love a liar?

MRS HUSHABYE. I dont know. But you can, fortunately. Otherwise there wouldnt be much love in the world.

ELLIE. But to lie like that! To be a boaster! a coward!

MRS HUSHABYE [*rising in alarm*] Pettikins: none of that, if you please. If you hint the slightest doubt of Hector's courage, he will go straight off and do the most horribly dangerous things to convince himself that he isnt a coward. He has a dreadful trick of getting out of one third-floor window and coming in at another, just to test his nerve. He has a whole drawerful of Albert Medals for saving people's lives.

ELLIE. He never told me that.

MRS HUSHABYE. He never boasts of anything he really did: he cant bear it; and it makes him shy if anyone else does. All his stories are made-up stories.

ELLIE [*coming to her*] Do you mean that he is really brave, and really has adventures, and yet tells lies about things that he never did and that never happened?

MRS HUSHABYE. Yes, pettikins, I do. People dont have their virtues and vices in sets: they have them anyhow: all mixed.

ELLIE [*staring at her thoughtfully*] Theres something odd about this house, Hesione, and even about you. I dont know why I'm talking to you so calmly. I have a horrible fear that my heart is broken, but that heartbreak is not like what I thought it must be.

MRS HUSHABYE [*fondling her*] It's only life educating you, pettikins. How do you feel about Boss Mangan now?

ELLIE [*disengaging herself with an expression of distaste*] Oh, how can you remind me of him, Hesione?

MRS HUSHABYE. Sorry, dear. I think I hear Hector coming back. You dont mind now, do you, dear?

ELLIE. Not in the least. I am quite cured.

 Mazzini Dunn and Hector come in from the hall.

HECTOR [*as he opens the door and allows Mazzini to pass in*] One second more, and she would have been a dead woman!

MAZZINI. Dear! dear! what an escape! Ellie, my love: Mr Hushabye has just been telling me the most extraordinary –

ELLIE. Yes: Ive heard it [*She crosses to the other side of the room*].

HECTOR [*following her*] Not this one: I'll tell it to you after dinner. I think youll like it. The truth is, I made it up for you, and was looking forward to the pleasure of telling it to you. But in a moment of impatience at being turned out of the room, I threw it away on your father.

ELLIE [*turning at bay with her back to the carpenter's bench, scornfully self-possessed*] It was not thrown away. He believes it. I should not have believed it.

MAZZINI [*benevolently*] Ellie is very naughty, Mr Hushabye. Of course she does not really think that. [*He goes to the bookshelves, and inspects the titles of the volumes*].

Boss Mangan comes in from the hall, followed by the Captain. Mangan, carefully frock-coated as for church or for a directors' meeting, is about fifty-five, with a careworn, mistrustful expression, standing a little on an entirely imaginary dignity, with a dull complexion, straight, lustreless hair, and features so entirely commonplace that it is impossible to describe them.

CAPTAIN SHOTOVER [*to Mrs Hushabye, introducing the newcomer*] Says his name is Mangan. Not ablebodied.

MRS HUSHABYE [*graciously*] How do you do, Mr Mangan?

MANGAN [*shaking hands*] Very pleased.

CAPTAIN SHOTOVER. Dunn's lost his muscle, but recovered his nerve. Men seldom do after three attacks of delirium tremens [*he goes into the pantry*].

MRS HUSHABYE. I congratulate you, Mr Dunn.

MAZZINI [*dazed*] I am a lifelong teetotaler.

MRS HUSHABYE. You will find it far less trouble to let papa have his own way than try to explain.

MAZZINI. But three attacks of delirium tremens, really!

MRS HUSHABYE [*to Mangan*] Do you know my husband, Mr Mangan [*she indicates Hector*].

MANGAN [*going to Hector, who meets him with outstretched hand*] Very pleased. [*Turning to Ellie*] I hope, Miss Ellie, you have not found the journey down too fatiguing. [*They shake hands*].

MRS HUSHABYE. Hector: shew Mr Dunn his room.

HECTOR. Certainly. Come along, Mr Dunn. [*He takes Mazzini out*].

ELLIE. You havnt shewn me my room yet, Hesione.

MRS HUSHABYE. How stupid of me! Come along. Make yourself quite at home, Mr Mangan. Papa will entertain you. [*She calls to the Captain in the pantry*] Papa: come and explain the house to Mr Mangan.

She goes out with Ellie. The Captain comes from the pantry.

CAPTAIN SHOTOVER. Youre going to marry Dunn's daughter. Dont. Youre too old.

MANGAN [*staggered*] Well! Thats fairly blunt, Captain.

CAPTAIN SHOTOVER. It's true.

MANGAN. She doesnt think so.

CAPTAIN SHOTOVER. She does.

MANGAN. Older men than I have –

CAPTAIN SHOTOVER [*finishing the sentence for him*] – made fools of themselves. That, also, is true.

MANGAN [*asserting himself*] I dont see that this is any business of yours.

CAPTAIN SHOTOVER. It is everybody's business. The stars in their courses are shaken when such things happen.

MANGAN. I'm going to marry her all the same.

CAPTAIN SHOTOVER. How do you know?

MANGAN [*playing the strong man*] I intend to. I mean to. See? I never made up my mind to do a thing yet that I didnt bring it off. Thats the sort of man I am; and there will be a better understanding between us when you make up your mind to that, Captain.

CAPTAIN SHOTOVER. You frequent picture palaces.

MANGAN. Perhaps I do. Who told you?

CAPTAIN SHOTOVER. Talk like a man, not like a movy. You mean that you make a hundred thousand a year.

MANGAN. I dont boast. But when I meet a man that makes a hundred thousand a year, I take off my hat to that man, and stretch out my hand to him and call him brother.

CAPTAIN SHOTOVER. Then you also make a hundred thousand a year, hey?

MANGAN. No. I cant say that. Fifty thousand, perhaps.

CAPTAIN SHOTOVER. His half brother only [*he turns away from Mangan with his usual abruptness, and collects the empty tea-cups on the Chinese tray*].

MANGAN [*irritated*] See here, Captain Shotover. I dont quite understand my position here. I came here on your daughter's invitation. Am I in her house or in yours?

CAPTAIN SHOTOVER. You are beneath the dome of heaven, in the house of God. What is true within these walls is true outside them. Go out on the seas; climb the mountains; wander through the valleys. She is still too young.

MANGAN [*weakening*] But I'm very little over fifty.

CAPTAIN SHOTOVER. You are still less under sixty. Boss Mangan: you will not marry the pirate's child [*he carries the tray away into the pantry*].

MANGAN [*following him to the half door*] What pirate's child? What are you talking about?

CAPTAIN SHOTOVER [*in the pantry*] Ellie Dunn. You will not marry her.

MANGAN. Who will stop me?

CAPTAIN SHOTOVER [*emerging*] My daughter [*he makes for the door leading to the hall*].

MANGAN [*following him*] Mrs Hushabye! Do you mean to say she brought me down here to break it off?

CAPTAIN SHOTOVER [*stopping and turning on him*] I know nothing more than I have seen in her eye. She will break it off. Take my advice: marry a West Indian negress: they make excellent wives. I was married to one myself for two years.

MANGAN. Well, I am damned!

CAPTAIN SHOTOVER. I thought so. I was, too, for many years. The negress redeemed me.

MANGAN [*feebly*] This is queer. I ought to walk out of this house.

CAPTAIN SHOTOVER. Why?

MANGAN. Well, many men would be offended by your style of talking.

CAPTAIN SHOTOVER. Nonsense! It's the other sort of talking that makes quarrels. Nobody ever quarrels with me.

A gentleman, whose firstrate tailoring and frictionless manners proclaim the wellbred West Ender, comes in from the hall. He has an engaging air of being young and unmarried, but on close inspection is found to be at least over forty.

THE GENTLEMAN. Excuse my intruding in this fashion; but there is no knocker on the door; and the bell does not seem to ring.

CAPTAIN SHOTOVER. Why should there be a knocker? Why should the bell ring? The door is open.

THE GENTLEMAN. Precisely. So I ventured to come in.

CAPTAIN SHOTOVER. Quite right. I will see about a room for you [*he makes for the door*].

THE GENTLEMAN [*stopping him*] But I'm afraid you don't know who I am.

CAPTAIN SHOTOVER. Do you suppose that at my age I make distinctions between one fellowcreature and another? [*He goes out. Mangan and the newcomer stare at one another*].

MANGAN. Strange character, Captain Shotover, sir.

THE GENTLEMAN. Very.

CAPTAIN SHOTOVER [*shouting outside*] Hesione: another person has arrived and wants a room. Man about town, well dressed, fifty.

THE GENTLEMAN. Fancy Hesione's feelings! May I ask are you a member of the family?

MANGAN. No.

THE GENTLEMAN. I am. At least a connexion.

Mrs Hushabye comes back.

MRS HUSHABYE. How do you do? How good of you to come!

THE GENTLEMAN. I am very glad indeed to make your acquaintance, Hesione. [*Instead of taking her hand he kisses her. At the same moment the Captain appears in the doorway*]. You will excuse my kissing your daughter, Captain, when I tell you that –

CAPTAIN SHOTOVER. Stuff! Everyone kisses my daughter. Kiss her as much as you like [*he makes for the pantry*].

THE GENTLEMAN. Thank you. One moment. Captain. [*The Captain halts and turns. The gentleman goes to him affably*]. Do you happen to remember – but probably you dont, as it occurred many years ago – that your younger daughter married a numskull.

CAPTAIN SHOTOVER. Yes. She said she'd marry anybody to get away from this house. I should not have recognized you: your head is no longer like a walnut. Your aspect is softened. You have been boiled in bread and milk for years and years, like other married men. Poor devil! [*He disappears into the pantry*].

MRS HUSHABYE [*going past Mangan to the gentleman and scrutinizing him*] I dont believe you are Hastings Utterword.

THE GENTLEMAN. I am not.

MRS HUSHABYE. Then what business had you to kiss me?

THE GENTLEMAN. I thought I would like to. The fact is, I am Randall Utterword, the unworthy younger brother of Hastings. I was abroad diplomatizing when he was married.

LADY UTTERWORD [*dashing in*] Hesione: where is the key of the wardrobe in my room? My diamonds are in my dressing-bag: I must lock it up – [*recognizing the stranger with a shock*] Randall: how dare you? [*She marches at him past Mrs Hushabye, who retreats and joins Mangan near the sofa*].

RANDALL. How dare I what? I am not doing anything.

LADY UTTERWORD. Who told you I was here?

RANDALL. Hastings. You had just left when I called on you at Claridge's; so I followed you down here. You are looking extremely well.

LADY UTTERWORD. Dont presume to tell me so.

MRS HUSHABYE. What is wrong with Mr Randall, Addy?

LADY UTTERWORD [*recollecting herself*] Oh, nothing. But he has no right to come bothering you and papa without being invited [*she goes to the window-seat and sits down, turning away from them ill-humoredly and looking into the garden, where Hector and Ellie are now seen strolling together*].

MRS HUSHABYE. I think you have not met Mr Mangan, Addy.

LADY UTTERWORD [*turning her head and nodding coldly to Mangan*] I beg your pardon. Randall: you have flustered me so: I made a perfect fool of myself.

MRS HUSHABYE. Lady Utterword. My sister. My younger sister.

MANGAN [*bowing*] Pleased to meet you, Lady Utterword.

LADY UTTERWORD [*with marked interest*] Who is that gentleman walking in the garden with Miss Dunn?

MRS HUSHABYE. I don't know. She quarrelled mortally with my husband only ten minutes ago; and I didn't know anyone else had come. It must be a visitor. [*She goes to the window to look*]. Oh, it is Hector. Theyve made it up.

LADY UTTERWORD. Your husband! That handsome man?

MRS HUSHABYE. Well, why shouldnt my husband be a handsome man?

RANDALL [*joining them at the window*] One's husband never is, Ariadne [*he sits by Lady Utterword, on her right*].

MRS HUSHABYE. One's sister's husband always is, Mr Randall.

LADY UTTERWORD. Dont be vulgar, Randall. And you, Hesione, are just as bad.

Ellie and Hector come in from the garden by the starboard door. Randall rises. Ellie retires into the corner near the pantry. Hector comes forward; and Lady Utterword rises looking her very best.

MRS HUSHABYE. Hector: this is Addy.

HECTOR [*apparently surprised*] Not this lady.

LADY UTTERWORD [*smiling*] Why not?

HECTOR [*looking at her with a piercing glance of deep but respectful admiration, his moustache bristling*] I thought – [*pulling himself together*] I beg your pardon, Lady Utterword. I am extremely glad to welcome you at last under our roof [*he offers his hand with grave courtesy*].

MRS HUSHABYE. She wants to be kissed, Hector.

LADY UTTERWORD. Hesione! [*but she still smiles*].

MRS HUSHABYE. Call her Addy; and kiss her like a good brother-in-law; and have done with it. [*She leaves them to themselves*].

HECTOR. Behave yourself, Hesione. Lady Utterword is entitled not only to hospitality but to civilization.

LADY UTTERWORD [*gratefully*] Thank you, Hector. [*They shake hands cordially*].

Mazzini Dunn is seen crossing the garden from starboard to port.

CAPTAIN SHOTOVER [*coming from the pantry and addressing Ellie*] Your father has washed himself.

ELLIE [*quite self-possessed*] He often does, Captain Shotover.

CAPTAIN SHOTOVER. A strange conversion! I saw him through the pantry window.

Mazzini Dunn enters through the port window door, newly washed and brushed, and stops, smiling benevolently, between Mangan and Mrs Hushabye.

MRS HUSHABYE [*introducing*] Mr Mazzini Dunn, Lady Ut— oh, I forgot: youve met. [*Indicating Ellie*] Miss Dunn.

MAZZINI [*walking across the room to take Ellie's hand, and beaming at his own naughty irony*] I have met Miss Dunn also. She is my daughter. [*He draws her arm through his caressingly*].

MRS HUSHABYE. Of course: how stupid! Mr Utterword, my sister's – er –

RANDALL [*shaking hands agreeably*] Her brother-in-law, Mr Dunn. How do you do?

MRS HUSHABYE. This is my husband.

HECTOR. We have met, dear. Dont introduce us any more. [*He moves away to the big chair, and adds*] Wont you sit down, Lady Utterword? [*She does so very graciously*].

MRS HUSHABYE. Sorry. I hate it: it's like making people shew their tickets.

MAZZINI [*sententiously*] How little it tells us, after all! The great question is, not who we are, but what we are.

CAPTAIN SHOTOVER. Ha! What are you?

MAZZINI [*taken aback*] What am I?

CAPTAIN SHOTOVER. A thief, a pirate, and a murderer.

MAZZINI. I assure you you are mistaken.

CAPTAIN SHOTOVER. An adventurous life; but what does it end in? Respectability. A ladylike daughter. The language and appearance of a city missionary. Let it be a warning to all of you [*he goes out through the garden*].

DUNN. I hope nobody here believes that I am a thief, a pirate, or a murderer. Mrs Hushabye: will you excuse me a moment? I must really go and explain. [*He follows the Captain*].

MRS HUSHABYE [*as he goes*] It's no use. Youd really better – [*but Dunn has vanished*]. We had better all go out and look for some tea. We never have regular tea; but you can always get some when you want: the servants keep it stewing all day. The kitchen veranda is the best place to ask. May I shew you? [*She goes to the starboard door*].

RANDALL [*going with her*] Thank you, I dont think I'll take any tea this afternoon. But if you will shew me the garden – ?

MRS HUSHABYE. Theres nothing to see in the garden except papa's observatory, and a gravel pit with a cave where he keeps dynamite and things of that sort. However, it's pleasanter out of doors; so come along.

RANDALL. Dynamite! Isnt that rather risky?

MRS HUSHABYE. Well, we dont sit in the gravel pit when theres a thunderstorm.

LADY UTTERWORD. Thats something new. What is the dynamite for?

HECTOR. To blow up the human race if it goes too far. He is trying to discover a psychic ray that will explode all the explosives at the will of a Mahatma.

ELLIE. The Captain's tea is delicious, Mr Utterword.

MRS HUSHABYE [*stopping in the doorway*] Do you mean to say that youve had some of my father's tea? that you got round him before you were ten minutes in the house?

ELLIE. I did.

MRS HUSHABYE. You little devil! [*She goes out with Randall*].

MANGAN. Wont you come, Miss Ellie?

ELLIE. I'm too tired. I'll take a book up to my room and rest a little. [*She goes to the bookshelf*].

MANGAN. Right. You cant do better. But I'm disappointed. [*He follows Randall and Mrs Hushabye*].

   Ellie, Hector, and Lady Utterword are left. Hector is close to Lady Utterword. They look at Ellie, waiting for her to go.

ELLIE [*looking at the title of a book*] Do you like stories of adventure, Lady Utterword?

LADY UTTERWORD [*patronizingly*] Of course, dear.

ELLIE. Then I'll leave you to Mr Hushabye. [*She goes out through the hall*].

HECTOR. That girl is mad about tales of adventure. The lies I have to tell her!

LADY UTTERWORD [*not interested in Ellie*] When you saw me what did you mean by saying that you thought, and then stopping short? What did you think?

HECTOR [*folding his arms and looking down at her magnetically*] May I tell you?

LADY UTTERWORD. Of course.

HECTOR. It will not sound very civil. I was on the point of saying 'I thought you were a plain woman.'

LADY UTTERWORD. Oh for shame, Hector! What right had you to notice whether I am plain or not?

HECTOR. Listen to me, Ariadne. Until today I have seen only photographs of you; and no photograph can give the strange fascination of the daughters of that supernatural old man. There is some damnable quality in them that destroys men's moral sense, and carries them beyond honor and dishonor. You know that, dont you?

LADY UTTERWORD. Perhaps I do, Hector. But let me warn you once for all that I am a rigidly conventional woman. You may think because I'm a Shotover that I'm a Bohemian, because we are all so horribly Bohemian. But I'm not. I hate and loathe Bohemianism. No child brought up in a strict Puritan household ever suffered from Puritanism as I suffered from our Bohemianism.

HECTOR. Our children are like that. They spend their holidays in the houses of their respectable schoolfellows.

LADY UTTERWORD. I shall invite them for Christmas.

HECTOR. Their absence leaves us both without our natural chaperons.

LADY UTTERWORD. Children are certainly very inconvenient sometimes. But intelligent people can always manage, unless they are Bohemians.

HECTOR. You are no Bohemian; but you are no Puritan either: your attraction is alive and powerful. What sort of woman do you count yourself?

LADY UTTERWORD. I am a woman of the world, Hector; and I can assure you that if you will only take the trouble always to do the perfectly correct thing, and to say the perfectly correct thing, you can do just what you like. An ill-conducted, careless woman gets simply no chance. An ill-conducted, careless man is never allowed within arm's length of any woman worth knowing.

HECTOR. I see. You are neither a Bohemian woman nor a Puritan woman. You are a dangerous woman.

LADY UTTERWORD. On the contrary, I am a safe woman.

HECTOR. You are a most accursedly attractive woman. Mind: I am not making love to you. I do not like being attracted. But you had better know how I feel if you are going to stay here.

LADY UTTERWORD. You are an exceedingly clever lady-killer, Hector. And terribly handsome. I am quite a good player, myself, at that game. Is it quite understood that we are only playing?

HECTOR. Quite. I am deliberately playing the fool, out of sheer worthlessness.

LADY UTTERWORD [*rising brightly*] Well, you are my brother-in-law. Hesione asked you to kiss me. [*He seizes her in his arms, and kisses her strenuously*]. Oh! that was a little more than play, brother-in-law. [*She pushes him suddenly away*]. You shall not do that again.

HECTOR. In effect, you got your claws deeper into me than I intended.

MRS HUSHABYE [*coming in from the garden*] Dont let me disturb you: I only want a cap to put on daddiest. The sun is setting; and he'll catch cold [*she makes for the door leading to the hall*].

LADY UTTERWORD. Your husband is quite charming, darling. He has actually condescended to kiss me at last. I shall go into the garden: it's cooler now [*she goes out by the port door*].

MRS HUSHABYE. Take care, dear child. I dont believe any man can kiss Addy without falling in love with her. [*She goes into the hall*].

HECTOR [*striking himself on the chest*] Fool! Goat!

Mrs Hushabye comes back with the Captain's cap.

HECTOR. Your sister is an extremely enterprising old girl. Wheres Miss Dunn!

MRS HUSHABYE. Mangan says she has gone up to her room for a nap. Addy wont let you talk to Ellie: she has marked you for her own.

HECTOR. She has the diabolical family fascination. I began making love to her automatically. What am I to do? I cant fall in love; and I cant hurt a woman's feelings by telling her so when she falls in love with me. And as women are always falling in love with my moustache I get landed in all sorts of tedious and terrifying flirtations in which I'm not a bit in earnest.

MRS HUSHABYE. Oh, neither is Addy. She has never been in love in her life, though she has always been trying to fall in head over ears. She is worse than you, because you had one real go at least, with me.

HECTOR. That was a confounded madness. I cant believe that such an amazing experience is common. It has left its mark on me. I believe that is why I have never been able to repeat it.

MRS HUSHABYE [*laughing and caressing his arm*] We were frightfully in love with one another, Hector. It was such an enchanting dream that I have never been able to grudge it to you or anyone else since. I have invited all sorts of pretty women to the house on the chance of giving you another turn. But it has never come off.

HECTOR. I dont know that I want it to come off. It was damned dangerous. You fascinated me; but I loved you; so it was heaven. This sister of yours fascinates me; but I hate her; so it is hell. I shall kill her if she persists.

MRS HUSHABYE. Nothing will kill Addy: she is as strong as a horse. [*Releasing him*] Now *I* am going off to fascinate somebody.

HECTOR. The Foreign Office toff? Randall?

MRS HUSHABYE. Goodness gracious, no! Why should I fascinate him?

HECTOR. I presume you dont mean the bloated capitalist, Mangan?

MRS HUSHABYE. Hm! I think he had better be fascinated by me than by Ellie. [*She is going into the garden when the Captain comes in from it with some sticks in his hand*]. What have you got there, daddiest?

CAPTAIN SHOTOVER. Dynamite.

MRS HUSHABYE. Youve been to the gravel pit. Dont drop it about the house: theres a dear. [*She goes into the garden, where the evening light is now very red*].

HECTOR. Listen, O sage. How long dare you concentrate on a feeling without risking having it fixed in your consciousness all the rest of your life?

CAPTAIN SHOTOVER. Ninety minutes. An hour and a half. [*He goes into the pantry*].

Hector, left alone, contracts his brows, and falls into a daydream. He does not move for some time. Then he folds his arms. Then, throwing his hands behind him, and gripping one with the other, he strides tragically once to and fro. Suddenly he snatches his walking-stick from the teak table, and draws it; for it is a sword-stick. He fights a desperate duel with an imaginary antagonist, and after many vicissitudes runs him through the body up to the hilt. He sheathes his sword and throws it on the sofa, falling into another reverie as he does so. He looks straight into the eyes of an imaginary woman; seizes her by the arms; and says in a deep and thrilling tone 'Do you love me!' The Captain comes out of the pantry at this moment; and Hector, caught with his arms stretched out and his fists clenched, has to account for his attitude by going through a series of gymnastic exercises.

CAPTAIN SHOTOVER. That sort of strength is no good. You will never be as strong as a gorilla.

HECTOR. What is the dynamite for?

CAPTAIN SHOTOVER. To kill fellows like Mangan.

HECTOR. No use. They will always be able to buy more dynamite than you.

CAPTAIN SHOTOVER. I will make a dynamite that he cannot explode.

HECTOR: And that you can, eh?

CAPTAIN SHOTOVER. Yes: when I have attained the seventh degree of concentration.

HECTOR. Whats the use of that? You never do attain it.

CAPTAIN SHOTOVER. What then is to be done? Are we to be kept for ever in the mud by these hogs to whom the universe is nothing but a machine for greasing their bristles and filling their snouts?

HECTOR. Are Mangan's bristles worse than Randall's lovelocks?

CAPTAIN SHOTOVER. We must win powers of life and death over them both. I refuse to die until I have invented the means.

HECTOR. Who are we that we should judge them?

CAPTAIN SHOTOVER. What are they that they should judge us? Yet they do, unhesitatingly. There is an enmity between our seed and their seed. They know it and act on it, strangling our souls. They believe in themselves. When we believe in ourselves, we shall kill them.

HECTOR. It is the same seed. You forget that your pirate has a very nice daughter. Mangan's son may be a Plato: Randall's a Shelley. What was my father?

CAPTAIN SHOTOVER. The damndest scoundrel I ever met. [*He replaces the drawing-board; sits down at the table; and begins to mix a wash of color*].

HECTOR. Precisely. Well, dare you kill his innocent grandchildren?

86

CAPTAIN SHOTOVER. They are mine also.

HECTOR. Just so. We are members one of another. [*He throws himself carelessly on the sofa*]. I tell you I have often thought of this killing of human vermin. Many men have thought of it. Decent men are like Daniel in the lion's den: their survival is a miracle; and they do not always survive. We live among the Mangans and Randalls and Billie Dunns as they, poor devils, live among the disease germs and the doctors and the lawyers and the parsons and the restaurant chefs and the tradesmen and the servants and all the rest of the parasites and blackmailers. What are our terrors to theirs? Give me the power to kill them; and I'll spare them in sheer –

CAPTAIN SHOTOVER [*cutting in sharply*] Fellow feeling?

HECTOR. No. I should kill myself if I believed that. I must believe that my spark, small as it is, is divine, and that the red light over their door is hell fire. I should spare them in simple magnanimous pity.

CAPTAIN SHOTOVER. You cant spare them until you have the power to kill them. At present they have the power to kill you. There are millions of blacks over the water for them to train and let loose on us. Theyre going to do it. Theyre doing it already.

HECTOR. They are too stupid to use their power.

CAPTAIN SHOTOVER [*throwing down his brush and coming to the end of the sofa*] Do not deceive yourself: they do use it. We kill the better half of ourselves every day to propitiate them. The knowledge that these people are there to render all our aspirations barren prevents us having the aspirations. And when we are tempted to seek their destruction they bring forth demons to delude us, disguised as pretty daughters, and singers and poets and the like, for whose sake we spare them.

HECTOR [*sitting up and leaning towards him*] May not Hesione be such a demon, brought forth by you lest I should slay you?

CAPTAIN SHOTOVER. That is possible. She has used you up, and left you nothing but dreams, as some women do.

HECTOR. Vampire women, demon women.

CAPTAIN SHOTOVER. Men think the world well lost for them, and lose it accordingly. Who are the men that do things? The husbands of the shrew and of the drunkard, the men with the thorn in the flesh. [*Walking distractedly away towards the pantry*] I must think these things out. [*Turning suddenly*] But I go on with the dynamite none the less. I will discover a ray mightier than any X-ray: a mind ray that will explode the ammunition in the belt of my adversary before he can point his gun at me. And I must hurry. I am old: I have no time to waste in talk [*he is about to go into the pantry, and Hector is making for the hall, when Hesione comes back*].

MRS HUSHABYE. Daddiest: you and Hector must come and help me to entertain all these people. What on earth were you shouting about?

HECTOR [*stopping in the act of turning the doorhandle*] He is madder than usual.

MRS HUSHABYE. We all are.

HECTOR. I must change [*he resumes his door opening*].

MRS HUSHABYE. Stop, stop. Come back, both of you. Come back. [*They return, reluctantly*]. Money is running short.

HECTOR. Money! Where are my April dividends?

MRS HUSHABYE. Where is the snow that fell last year?

CAPTAIN SHOTOVER. Where is all the money you had for that patent lifeboat I invented?

MRS HUSHABYE. Five hundred pounds; and I have made it last since Easter!

CAPTAIN SHOTOVER. Since Easter! Barely four months! Monstrous extravagance! I could live for seven years on £500.

MRS HUSHABYE. Not keeping open house as we do here, daddiest.

CAPTAIN SHOTOVER. Only £500 for that lifeboat! I got twelve thousand for the invention before that.

MRS HUSHABYE. Yes, dear; but that was for the ship with the magnetic keel that sucked up submarines. Living at the rate we do, you cannot afford life-saving inventions. Cant you think of something that will murder half Europe at one bang?

CAPTAIN SHOTOVER. No. I am ageing fast. My mind does not dwell on slaughter as it did when I was a boy. Why doesnt your husband invent something? He does nothing but tell lies to women.

HECTOR. Well, that is a form of invention, is it not? However, you are right: I ought to support my wife.

MRS HUSHABYE. Indeed you shall do nothing of the sort: I should never see you from breakfast to dinner. I want my husband.

HECTOR [bitterly] I might as well be your lapdog.

MRS HUSHABYE. Do you want to be my breadwinner, like the other poor husbands?

HECTOR. No, by thunder! What a damned creature a husband is anyhow!

MRS HUSHABYE [to the Captain] What about that harpoon cannon?

CAPTAIN SHOTOVER. No use. It kills whales, not men.

MRS HUSHABYE. Why not? You fire the harpoon out of a cannon. It sticks in the enemy's general; you wind him in; and there you are.

HECTOR. You are your father's daughter, Hesione.

CAPTAIN SHOTOVER. There is something in it. Not to wind in generals: they are not dangerous. But one could fire a grapnel and wind in a machine gun or even a tank. I will think it out.

MRS HUSHABYE [squeezing the Captain's arm affectionately] Saved! You are a darling, daddiest. Now we must go back to these dreadful people and entertain them.

CAPTAIN SHOTOVER. They have had no dinner. Dont forget that.

HECTOR. Neither have I. And it is dark: it must be all hours.

MRS HUSHABYE. Oh, Guinness will produce some sort of dinner for them. The servants always take jolly good care that there is food in the house.

CAPTAIN SHOTOVER [*raising a strange wail in the darkness*] What a house! What a daughter!

MRS HUSHABYE [*raving*] What a father!

HECTOR [*following suit*] What a husband!

CAPTAIN SHOTOVER. Is there no thunder in heaven?

HECTOR. Is there no beauty, no bravery, on earth?

MRS HUSHABYE. What do men want? They have their food, their firesides, their clothes mended, and our love at the end of the day. Why are they not satisfied? Why do they envy us the pain with which we bring them into the world, and make strange dangers and torments for themselves to be even with us?

CAPTAIN SHOTOVER [*weirdly chanting*]

I built a house for my daughters, and opened the
    doors thereof,
That men might come for their choosing, and their betters spring from their love;
But one of them married a numskull;

HECTOR [*taking up the rhythm*]

The other a liar wed;

MRS HUSHABYE [*completing the stanza*]

And now must she lie beside him, even as she made her
    bed.

LADY UTTERWORD [*calling from the garden*] Hesione! Hesione! Where are you?

HECTOR. The cat is on the tiles.

MRS HUSHABYE. Coming, darling, coming [*she goes quickly into the garden*].

The Captain goes back to his place at the table.

HECTOR [*going into the hall*] Shall I turn up the lights for you?

CAPTAIN SHOTOVER. No. Give me deeper darkness. Money is not made in the light.

ACT II

The same room, with the lights turned up and the curtains drawn.
Ellie comes in, followed by Mangan. Both are dressed for dinner.
She strolls to the drawing-table. He comes between the table and the
wicker chair.

MANGAN. What a dinner! I dont call it a dinner: I call it a
meal.

ELLIE. I am accustomed to meals, Mr Mangan, and very
lucky to get them. Besides, the captain cooked some mac-
aroni for me.

MANGAN [*shuddering liverishly*] Too rich: I cant eat such
things. I suppose it's because I have to work so much with
my brain. Thats the worst of being a man of business: you
are always thinking, thinking, thinking. By the way, now
that we are alone, may I take the opportunity to come
to a little understanding with you?

ELLIE [*settling into the draughtsman's seat*] Certainly. I should
like to.

MANGAN [*taken aback*] Should you? That surprises me; for I
thought I noticed this afternoon that you avoided me all
you could. Not for the first time either.

ELLIE. I was very tired and upset. I wasnt used to the ways
of this extraordinary house. Please forgive me.

MANGAN. Oh, thats all right: I dont mind. But Captain
Shotover has been talking to me about you. You and me,
you know.

ELLIE [*interested*] The Captain! What did he say?

MANGAN. Well, he noticed the difference between our ages.

ELLIE. He notices everything.

MANGAN. You dont mind, then?

ELLIE. Of course I know quite well that our engagement –

92

MANGAN. Oh! you call it an engagement.

ELLIE. Well, isnt it?

MANGAN. Oh, yes, yes: no doubt it is if you hold to it. This is the first time youve used the word; and I didnt quite know where we stood: thats all. [*He sits down in the wicker chair; and resigns himself to allow her to lead the conversation*]. You were saying – ?

ELLIE. Was I? I forget. Tell me. Do you like this part of the country? I heard you ask Mr Hushabye at dinner whether there are any nice houses to let down here.

MANGAN. I like the place. The air suits me. I shouldnt be surprised if I settled down here.

ELLIE. Nothing would please me better. The air suits me too. And I want to be near Hesione.

MANGAN [*with growing uneasiness*] The air may suit us; but the question is, should we suit one another? Have you thought about that?

ELLIE. Mr Mangan: we must be sensible, mustnt we? It's no use pretending that we are Romeo and Juliet. But we can get on very well together if we choose to make the best of it. Your kindness of heart will make it easy for me.

MANGAN [*leaning forward, with the beginning of something like deliberate unpleasantness in his voice*] Kindness of heart, eh? I ruined your father, didnt I?

ELLIE. Oh, not intentionally.

MANGAN. Yes I did. Ruined him on purpose.

ELLIE. On purpose!

MANGAN. Not out of ill-nature, you know. And youll admit that I kept a job for him when I had finished with him. But business is business; and I ruined him as a matter of business.

ELLIE. I dont understand how that can be. Are you trying to make me feel that I need not be grateful to you, so that I may choose freely?

MANGAN [*rising aggressively*] No. I mean what I say.

ELLIE. But how could it possibly do you any good to ruin my father? The money he lost was yours.

MANGAN [*with a sour laugh*] Was mine! It is mine, Miss Ellie, and all the money the other fellows lost too. [*He shoves his hands into his pockets and shews his teeth*]. I just smoked them out like a hive of bees. What do you say to that? A bit of a shock, eh?

ELLIE. It would have been, this morning. Now! you cant think how little it matters. But it's quite interesting. Only, you must explain it to me. I dont understand it. [*Propping her elbows on the drawing-board and her chin on her hands, she composes herself to listen with a combination of conscious curiosity with unconscious contempt which provokes him to more and more unpleasantness, and an attempt at patronage of her ignorance*].

MANGAN. Of course you dont understand: what do you know about business? You just listen and learn. Your father's business was a new business; and I dont start new businesses: I let other fellows start them. They put all their money and their friends' money into starting them. They wear out their souls and bodies trying to make a success of them. Theyre what you call enthusiasts. But the first dead lift of the thing is too much for them; and they havnt enough financial experience. In a year or so they have either to let the whole show go bust, or sell out to a new lot of fellows for a few deferred ordinary shares: that is, if theyre lucky enough to get anything at all. As likely as not the very same thing happens to the new lot. They put in more money and a couple of years more work; and then perhaps they have to sell out to a third lot. If it's really a big thing the third lot will have to sell out too, and leave their work and their money behind them. And thats where the real business man comes in: where I come in. But I'm cleverer than some: I dont mind dropping a little money to start the process. I took your father's measure. I saw

94

that he had a sound idea, and that he would work himself silly for it if he got the chance. I saw that he was a child in business, and was dead certain to outrun his expenses and be in too great a hurry to wait for his market. I knew that the surest way to ruin a man who doesnt know how to handle money is to give him some. I explained my idea to some friends in the city, and they found the money; for I take no risks in ideas, even when theyre my own. Your father and the friends that ventured their money with him were no more to me than a heap of squeezed lemons. Youve been wasting your gratitude: my kind heart is all rot. I'm sick of it. When I see your father beaming at me with his moist, grateful eyes, regularly wallowing in gratitude, I sometimes feel I must tell him the truth or burst. What stops me is that I know he wouldnt believe me. He'd think it was my modesty, as you did just now. He'd think anything rather than the truth, which is that he's a blamed fool, and I am a man that knows how to take care of himself. [*He throws himself back into the big chair with large self-approval*]. Now what do you think of me, Miss Ellie?

ELLIE [*dropping her hands*] How strange! that my mother, who knew nothing at all about business, should have been quite right about you! She always said – not before papa, of course, but to us children – that you were just that sort of man.

MANGAN [*sitting up, much hurt*] Oh! did she? And yet she'd have let you marry me.

ELLIE. Well, you see, Mr Mangan, my mother married a very good man – for whatever you may think of my father as a man of business, he is the soul of goodness – and she is not at all keen on my doing the same.

MANGAN. Anyhow, you dont want to marry me now, do you?

ELLIE [*very calmly*] Oh, I think so. Why not?

MANGAN [*rising aghast*] Why not!

ELLIE. I dont see why we shouldnt get on very well together.

MANGAN. Well, but look here, you know – [*he stops, quite at a loss*].

ELLIE [*patiently*] Well?

MANGAN. Well, I thought you were rather particular about people's characters.

ELLIE. If we women were particular about men's characters, we should never get married at all, Mr Mangan.

MANGAN. A child like you talking of 'we women'! What next! Youre not in earnest?

ELLIE. Yes I am. Arnt you?

MANGAN. You mean to hold me to it?

ELLIE. Do you wish to back out of it?

MANGAN. Oh no. Not exactly back out of it.

ELLIE. Well?

He has nothing to say. With a long whispered whistle, he drops into the wicker chair and stares before him like a beggared gambler. But a cunning look soon comes into his face. He leans over towards her on his right elbow, and speaks in a low steady voice.

MANGAN. Suppose I told you I was in love with another woman!

ELLIE [*echoing him*] Suppose I told you I was in love with another man!

MANGAN [*bouncing angrily out of his chair*] I'm not joking.

ELLIE. Who told you *I* was?

MANGAN. I tell you I'm serious. Youre too young to be serious; but youll have to believe me. I want to be near your friend Mrs Hushabye. I'm in love with her. Now the murder's out.

ELLIE. I want to be near your friend Mr Hushabye. I'm in love with him. [*She rises and adds with a frank air*] Now we are in one another's confidence, we shall be real friends. Thank you for telling me.

MANGAN [*almost beside himself*] Do you think I'll be made a convenience of like this?

ELLIE. Come, Mr Mangan! you made a business convenience of my father. Well, a woman's business is marriage.
Why shouldnt I make a domestic convenience of you?

MANGAN. Because I dont choose, see? Because I'm not a
silly gull like your father. Thats why.

ELLIE [*with serene contempt*] You are not good enough to clean
my father's boots, Mr Mangan; and I am paying you a
great compliment in condescending to make a convenience
of you, as you call it. Of course you are free to throw over
our engagement if you like; but, if you do, youll never
enter Hesione's house again: I will take care of that.

MANGAN [*gasping*] You little devil, youve done me [*On the
point of collapsing into the big chair again he recovers himself*]
Wait a bit, though: youre not so cute as you think. You
cant beat Boss Mangan as easy as that. Suppose I go
straight to Mrs Hushabye and tell her that youre in love
with her husband.

ELLIE. She knows it.

MANGAN. You told her!!!

ELLIE. She told me.

MANGAN [*clutching at his bursting temples*] Oh, this is a crazy
house. Or else I'm going clean off my chump. Is she making a swop with you – she to have your husband and you
to have hers?

ELLIE. Well, you dont want us both, do you?

MANGAN [*throwing himself into the chair distractedly*] My brain
wont stand it. My head's going to split. Help! Help me to
hold it. Quick: hold it: squeeze it. Save me. [*Ellie comes behind his chair; clasps his head hard for a moment; then begins to
draw her hands from his forehead back to his ears*]. Thank you.
[*Drowsily*] Thats very refreshing. [*Waking a little*] Dont
you hypnotize me, though. Ive seen men made fools of by
hypnotism.

ELLIE [*steadily*] Be quiet. Ive seen men made fools of without hypnotism.

MANGAN [*humbly*] You dont dislike touching me, I hope. You never touched me before, I noticed.

ELLIE. Not since you fell in love naturally with a grown-up nice woman, who will never expect you to make love to her. And I will never expect him to make love to me.

MANGAN. He may, though.

ELLIE [*making her passes rhythmically*] Hush. Go to sleep. Do you hear? You are to go to sleep, go to sleep, go to sleep; be quiet, deeply deeply quiet; sleep, sleep, sleep, sleep, sleep.

He falls asleep. Ellie steals away; turns the light out; and goes into the garden.

Nurse Guinness opens the door and is seen in the light which comes in from the hall.

GUINNESS [*speaking to someone outside*] Mr Mangan's not here, ducky: theres no one here. It's all dark.

MRS HUSHABYE [*without*] Try the garden. Mr Dunn and I will be in my boudoir. Shew him the way.

GUINNESS. Yes, ducky. [*She makes for the garden door in the dark; stumbles over the sleeping Mangan; and screams*] Ahoo! Oh Lord, sir! I beg your pardon, I'm sure: I didnt see you in the dark. Who is it? [*She goes back to the door and turns on the light*]. Oh, Mr Mangan, sir, I hope I havnt hurt you plumping into your lap like that. [*Coming to him*] I was looking for you, sir. Mrs Hushabye says will you please – [*noticing that he remains quite insensible*] Oh, my good Lord, I hope I havnt killed him. Sir! Mr Mangan! Sir! [*She shakes him; and he is rolling inertly off the chair on the floor when she holds him up and props him against the cushion*]. Miss Hessy! Miss Hessy! Quick, doty darling. Miss Hessy! [*Mrs Hushabye comes in from the hall, followed by Mazzini Dunn*]. Oh, Miss Hessy, Ive been and killed him.

Mazzini runs round the back of the chair to Mangan's right hand, and sees that the nurse's words are apparently only too true.

MAZZINI. What tempted you to commit such a crime, woman?

MRS HUSHABYE [*trying not to laugh*] Do you mean you did it on purpose?

GUINNESS. Now is it likely I'd kill any man on purpose. I fell over him in the dark; and I'm a pretty tidy weight. He never spoke nor moved until I shook him; and then he would have dropped dead on the floor. Isnt it tiresome?

MRS HUSHABYE [*going past the nurse to Mangan's side, and inspecting him less credulously than Mazzini*] Nonsense! he is not dead: he is only asleep. I can see him breathing.

GUINNESS. But why wont he wake?

MAZZINI [*speaking very politely into Mangan's ear*] Mangan! My dear Mangan! [*he blows into Mangan's ear*].

MRS HUSHABYE. Thats no good [*she shakes him vigorously*]. Mr Mangan: wake up. Do you hear? [*He begins to roll over*]. Oh! Nurse, nurse: he's falling: help me.

    Nurse Guinness rushes to the rescue. With Mazzini's assistance, Mangan is propped safely up again.

GUINNESS [*behind the chair; bending over to test the case with her nose*] Would he be drunk, do you think, pet?

MRS HUSHABYE. Had he any of papa's rum?

MAZZINI. It cant be that: he is most abstemious. I am afraid he drank too much formerly, and has to drink too little now. You know, Mrs Hushabye, I really think he has been hypnotized.

GUINNESS. Hip no what, sir?

MAZZINI. One evening at home, after we had seen a hypnotizing performance, the children began playing at it; and Ellie stroked my head. I assure you I went off dead asleep; and they had to send for a professional to wake me up after I had slept eighteen hours. They had to carry me upstairs; and as the poor children were not very strong, they let me slip; and I rolled right down the whole flight and never woke up. [*Mrs Hushabye splutters*]. Oh, you may laugh, Mrs Hushabye; but I might have been killed.

MRS HUSHABYE. I couldnt have helped laughing even if you

had been, Mr Dunn. So Ellie has hypnotized him. What fun!

MAZZINI. Oh no, no, no. It was such a terrible lesson to her: nothing would induce her to try such a thing again.

MRS HUSHABYE. Then who did it? *I* didnt.

MAZZINI. I thought perhaps the Captain might have done it unintentionally. He is so fearfully magnetic: I feel vibrations whenever he comes close to me.

GUINNESS. The Captain will get him out of it anyhow, sir: I'll back him for that. I'll go fetch him [*she makes for the pantry*].

MRS HUSHABYE. Wait a bit. [*To Mazzini*] You say he is all right for eighteen hours?

MAZZINI. Well, *I* was asleep for eighteen hours.

MRS HUSHABYE. Were you any the worse for it?

MAZZINI. I dont quite remember. They had poured brandy down my throat, you see; and –

MRS HUSHABYE. Quite. Anyhow, you survived. Nurse, darling: go and ask Miss Dunn to come to us here. Say I want to speak to her particularly. You will find her with Mr Hushabye probably.

GUINNESS. I think not, ducky: Miss Addy is with him. But I'll find her and send her to you. [*She goes out into the garden*].

MRS HUSHABYE [*calling Mazzini's attention to the figure on the chair*] Now, Mr Dunn, look. Just look. Look hard. Do you still intend to sacrifice your daughter to that thing?

MAZZINI [*troubled*] You have completely upset me, Mrs Hushabye, by all you have said to me. That anyone could imagine that I – *I*, a consecrated soldier of freedom, if I may say so – could sacrifice Ellie to anybody or anyone, or that I should ever have dreamed of forcing her inclinations in any way, is a most painful blow to my – well, I suppose you would say to my good opinion of myself.

MRS HUSHABYE [*rather stolidly*] Sorry.

MAZZINI [*looking forlornly at the body*] What is your objection
to poor Mangan, Mrs Hushabye? He looks all right to me.
But then I am so accustomed to him.

MRS HUSHABYE. Have you no heart? Have you no sense?
Look at the brute! Think of poor weak innocent Ellie in
the clutches of this slavedriver, who spends his life making
thousands of rough violent workmen bend to his will and
sweat for him: a man accustomed to have great masses of
iron beaten into shape for him by steam-hammers! to
fight with women and girls over a halfpenny an hour
ruthlessly! a captain of industry, I think you call him,
dont you? Are you going to fling your delicate, sweet,
helpless child into such a beast's claws just because he will
keep her in an expensive house and make her wear diamonds to shew how rich he is?

MAZZINI [*staring at her in wide-eyed amazement*] Bless you, dear
Mrs Hushabye, what romantic ideas of business you have!
Poor dear Mangan isnt a bit like that.

MRS HUSHABYE [*scornfully*] Poor dear Mangan indeed!

MAZZINI. But he doesnt know anything about machinery.
He never goes near the men: he couldnt manage them:
he is afraid of them. I never can get him to take the least
interest in the works: he hardly knows more about them
than you do. People are cruelly unjust to Mangan: they
think he is all rugged strength just because his manners
are bad.

MRS HUSHABYE. Do you mean to tell me he isnt strong
enough to crush poor little Ellie?

MAZZINI. Of course it's very hard to say how any marriage
will turn out; but speaking for myself, I should say that
he wont have a dog's chance against Ellie. You know,
Ellie has remarkable strength of character. I think it is
because I taught her to like Shakespear when she was very
young.

MRS HUSHABYE [*contemptuously*] Shakespear! The next thing you will tell me is that you could have made a great deal more money than Mangan. [*She retires to the sofa, and sits down at the port end of it in the worst of humors*].

MAZZINI [*following her and taking the other end*] No: I'm no good at making money. I dont care enough for it, somehow. I'm not ambitious! that must be it. Mangan is wonderful about money: he thinks of nothing else. He is so dreadfully afraid of being poor. I am always thinking of other things: even at the works I think of the things we are doing and not of what they cost. And the worst of it is, poor Mangan doesnt know what to do with his money when he gets it. He is such a baby that he doesnt know even what to eat and drink: he has ruined his liver eating and drinking the wrong things; and now he can hardly eat at all. Ellie will diet him splendidly. You will be surprised when you come to know him better: he is really the most helpless of mortals. You get quite a protective feeling towards him.

MRS HUSHABYE. Then who manages his business, pray?

MAZZINI. I do. And of course other people like me.

MRS HUSHABYE. Footling people, you mean.

MAZZINI. I suppose youd think us so.

MRS HUSHABYE. And pray why dont you do without him if youre all so much cleverer?

MAZZINI. Oh, we couldnt: we should ruin the business in a year. I've tried; and I know. We should spend too much on everything. We should improve the quality of the goods and make them too dear. We should be sentimental about the hard cases among the workpeople. But Mangan keeps us in order. He is down on us about every extra halfpenny. We could never do without him. You see, he will sit up all night thinking of how to save sixpence. Wont Ellie make him jump, though, when she takes his house in hand!

MRS HUSHABYE. Then the creature is a fraud even as a captain of industry!

MAZZINI. I am afraid all the captains of industry are what you call frauds, Mrs Hushabye. Of course there are some manufacturers who really do understand their own works; but they dont make as high a rate of profit as Mangan does. I assure you Mangan is quite a good fellow in his way. He means well.

MRS HUSHABYE. He doesnt look well. He is not in his first youth, is he?

MAZZINI. After all, no husband is in his first youth for very long, Mrs Hushabye. And men cant afford to marry in their first youth nowadays.

MRS HUSHABYE. Now if *I* said that, it would sound witty. Why cant you say it wittily? What on earth is the matter with you? Why dont you inspire everybody with confidence? with respect?

MAZZINI [*humbly*] I think that what is the matter with me is that I am poor. You dont know what that means at home. Mind: I dont say they have ever complained. Theyve all been wonderful: theyve been proud of my poverty. Theyve even joked about it quite often. But my wife has had a very poor time of it. She has been quite resigned –

MRS HUSHABYE [*shuddering involuntarily*]!!

MAZZINI. There! You see, Mrs Hushabye. I dont want Ellie to live on resignation.

MRS HUSHABYE. Do you want her to have to resign herself to living with a man she doesnt love?

MAZZINI [*wistfully*] Are you sure that would be worse than living with a man she did love, if he was a footling person?

MRS HUSHABYE [*relaxing her contemptuous attitude, quite interested in Mazzini now*] You know, I really think you must love Ellie very much; for you become quite clever when you talk about her.

MAZZINI. I didnt know I was so very stupid on other subjects.

MRS HUSHABYE. You are, sometimes.

MAZZINI [*turning his head away; for his eyes are wet*] I have learnt a good deal about myself from you, Mrs Hushabye; and I'm afraid I shall not be the happier for your plain speaking. But if you thought I needed it to make me think of Ellie's happiness you were very much mistaken.

MRS HUSHABYE [*leaning towards him kindly*] Have I been a beast?

MAZZINI [*pulling himself together*] It doesnt matter about me, Mrs Hushabye. I think you like Ellie; and that is enough for me.

MRS HUSHABYE. I'm beginning to like you a little. I perfectly loathed you at first. I thought you the most odious, self-satisfied, boresome elderly prig I ever met.

MAZZINI [*resigned, and now quite cheerful*] I daresay I am all that. I never have been a favorite with gorgeous women like you. They always frighten me.

MRS HUSHABYE [*pleased*] Am I a gorgeous woman, Mazzini? I shall fall in love with you presently.

MAZZINI [*with placid gallantry*] No you wont, Hesione. But you would be quite safe. Would you believe it that quite a lot of women have flirted with me because I am quite safe? But they get tired of me for the same reason.

MRS HUSHABYE [*mischievously*] Take care. You may not be so safe as you think.

MAZZINI. Oh yes, quite safe. You see, I have been in love really: the sort of love that only happens once. [*Softly*] Thats why Ellie is such a lovely girl.

MRS HUSHABYE. Well, really, you a r e coming out. Are you quite sure you wont let me tempt you into a second grand passion?

MAZZINI. Quite. It wouldnt be natural. The fact is, you dont strike on my box, Mrs Hushabye; and I certainly dont strike on yours.

MRS HUSHABYE. I see. Your marriage was a safety match.

MAZZINI. What a very witty application of the expression I
used! I should never have thought of it.

Ellie comes in from the garden, looking anything but happy.

MRS HUSHABYE [*rising*] Oh! here is Ellie at last. [*She goes
behind the sofa*].

ELLIE [*on the threshold of the starboard door*] Guinness said you
wanted me: you and papa.

MRS HUSHABYE. You have kept us waiting so long that it
almost came to – well, never mind. Your father is a very
wonderful man [*she ruffles his hair affectionately*]: the only
one I ever met who could resist me when I made myself
really agreeable. [*She comes to the big chair, on Mangan's
left*]. Come here. I have something to shew you. [*Ellie
strolls listlessly to the other side of the chair*]. Look.

ELLIE [*contemplating Mangan without interest*] I know. He is
only asleep. We had a talk after dinner; and he fell asleep
in the middle of it.

MRS HUSHABYE. You did it, Ellie. You put him asleep.

MAZZINI [*rising quickly and coming to the back of the chair*] Oh,
I hope not. Did you, Ellie?

ELLIE [*wearily*] He asked me to.

MAZZINI. But it's dangerous. You know what happened to
me.

ELLIE [*utterly indifferent*] Oh, I daresay I can wake him. If
not, somebody else can.

MRS HUSHABYE. It doesnt matter, anyhow, because I have
at last persuaded your father that you dont want to marry
him.

ELLIE [*suddenly coming out of her listlessness, much vexed*] But
why did you do that, Hesione? I do want to marry him. I
fully intend to marry him.

MAZZINI. Are you quite sure, Ellie? Mrs Hushabye has
made me feel that I may have been thoughtless and selfish about it.

ELLIE [*very clearly and steadily*] Papa. When Mrs Hushabye

takes it on herself to explain to you what I think or dont think, shut your ears tight; and shut your eyes too. Hesione knows nothing about me: she hasnt the least notion of the sort of person I am, and never will. I promise you I wont do anything I dont want to do and mean to do for my own sake.

MAZZINI. You are quite, quite sure?

ELLIE. Quite, quite sure. Now you must go away and leave me to talk to Mrs Hushabye.

MAZZINI. But I should like to hear. Shall I be in the way?

ELLIE [*inexorable*] I had rather talk to her alone.

MAZZINI [*affectionately*] Oh, well, I know what a nuisance parents are, dear. I will be good and go. [*He goes to the garden door*]. By the way, do you remember the address of that professional who woke me up? Dont you think I had better telegraph to him.

MRS HUSHABYE [*moving towards the sofa*] It's too late to telegraph tonight.

MAZZINI. I suppose so. I do hope he'll wake up in the course of the night. [*He goes out into the garden*].

ELLIE [*turning vigorously on Hesione the moment her father is out of the room*] Hesione: what the devil do you mean by making mischief with my father about Mangan?

MRS HUSHABYE [*promptly losing her temper*] Dont you dare speak to me like that, you little minx. Remember that you are in my house.

ELLIE. Stuff! Why dont you mind your own business? What is it to you whether I choose to marry Mangan or not?

MRS HUSHABYE. Do you suppose you can bully me, you miserable little matrimonial adventurer?

ELLIE. Every woman who hasnt any money is a matrimonial adventurer. It's easy for you to talk: you have never known what it is to want money; and you can pick up men as if they were daisies. I am poor and respectable –

MRS HUSHABYE [*interrupting*] Ho! respectable! How did you pick up Mangan? How did you pick up my husband? You have the audacity to tell me that I am a – a – a –

ELLIE. A siren. So you are. You were born to lead men by the nose: if you werent, Marcus would have waited for me, perhaps.

MRS HUSHABYE [*suddenly melting and half laughing*] Oh, my poor Ellie, my pettikins, my unhappy darling! I am so sorry about Hector. But what can I do? It's not my fault: I'd give him to you if I could.

ELLIE. I dont blame you for that.

MRS HUSHABYE. What a brute I was to quarrel with you and call you names! Do kiss me and say youre not angry with me.

ELLIE [*fiercely*] Oh, dont slop and gush and be sentimental. Dont you see that unless I can be hard – as hard as nails – I shall go mad. I dont care a damn about your calling me names: do you think a woman in my situation can feel a few hard words?

MRS HUSHABYE. Poor little woman! Poor little situation!

ELLIE. I suppose you think youre being sympathetic. You are just foolish and stupid and selfish. You see me getting a smasher right in the face that kills a whole part of my life: the best part that can never come again; and you think you can help me over it by a little coaxing and kissing. When I want all the strength I can get to lean on: something iron, something stony, I dont care how cruel it is, you go all mushy and want to slobber over me. I'm not angry; I'm not unfriendly; but for God's sake do pull yourself together; and dont think that because youre on velvet and always have been, women who are in hell can take it as easily as you.

MRS HUSHABYE [*shrugging her shoulders*] Very well. [*She sits down on the sofa in her old place*]. But I warn you that when I am neither coaxing and kissing nor laughing, I am just wondering how much longer I can stand living in this cruel, damnable world. You object to the siren: well, I drop the siren. You want to rest your wounded bosom against a grindstone. Well [*folding her arms*], here is the grindstone.

ELLIE [*sitting down beside her, appeased*] Thats better: you really have the trick of falling in with everyone's mood; but you dont understand, because you are not the sort of woman for whom there is only one man and only one chance.

MRS HUSHABYE. I certainly dont understand how your marrying that object [*indicating Mangan*] will console you for not being able to marry Hector.

ELLIE. Perhaps you dont understand why I was quite a nice girl this morning, and am now neither a girl nor particularly nice.

MRS HUSHABYE. Oh yes I do. It's because you have made up your mind to do something despicable and wicked.

ELLIE. I dont think so, Hesione. I must make the best of my ruined house.

MRS HUSHABYE. Pooh! Youll get over it. Your house isnt ruined.

ELLIE. Of course I shall get over it. You dont suppose I'm going to sit down and die of a broken heart, I hope, or be an old maid living on a pittance from the Sick and Indigent Roomkeepers' Association. But my heart is broken, all the same. What I mean by that is that I know that what has happened to me with Marcus will not happen to me ever again. In the world for me there is Marcus and a lot of other men of whom one is just the same as another. Well, if I cant have love, thats no reason why I should have poverty. If Mangan has nothing else, he has money.

MRS HUSHABYE. And are there no young men with money?

ELLIE. Not within my reach. Besides, a young man would have the right to expect love from me, and would perhaps leave me when he found I could not give it to him. Rich young men can get rid of their wives, you know, pretty cheaply. But this object, as you call him, can expect nothing more from me than I am prepared to give him.

MRS HUSHABYE. He will be your owner, remember. If he buys you, he will make the bargain pay him and not you. Ask your father.

ELLIE [*rising and strolling to the chair to contemplate their subject*] You need not trouble on that score, Hesione. I have more to give Boss Mangan than he has to give me: it is I who am buying him, and at a pretty good price too, I think. Women are better at that sort of bargain than men. I have taken the Boss's measure; and ten Boss Mangans shall not prevent me doing far more as I please as his wife than I have ever been able to do as a poor girl. [*Stooping to the recumbent figure*] Shall they, Boss? I think not. [*She passes on to the drawing-table, and leans against the end of it, facing the windows*]. I shall not have to spend most of my time wondering how long my gloves will last, anyhow.

MRS HUSHABYE [*rising superbly*] Ellie: you are a wicked sordid little beast. And to think that I actually condescended to fascinate that creature there to save you from him! Well, let me tell you this: if you make this disgusting match, you will never see Hector again if I can help it.

ELLIE [*unmoved*] I nailed Mangan by telling him that if he did not marry me he should never see you again [*she lifts herself on her wrists and seats herself on the end of the table*].

MRS HUSHABYE [*recoiling*] Oh!

ELLIE. So you see I am not unprepared for your playing that trump against me. Well, you just try it: thats all. I should have made a man of Marcus, not a household pet.

MRS HUSHABYE [*flaming*] You dare!

ELLIE [*looking almost dangerous*] Set him thinking about me if you dare.

MRS HUSHABYE. Well, of all the impudent little fiends I ever met! Hector says there is a certain point at which the only answer you can give to a man who breaks all the rules is to knock him down. What would you say if I were to box your ears?

ELLIE [*calmly*] I should pull your hair.

MRS HUSHABYE [*mischievously*] That wouldnt hurt me. Perhaps it comes off at night.

ELLIE [*so taken aback that she drops off the table and runs to her*] Oh, you dont mean to say, Hesione, that your beautiful black hair is false?

MRS HUSHABYE [*patting it*] Dont tell Hector. He believes in it.

ELLIE [*groaning*] Oh! Even the hair that ensnared him false! Everything false!

MRS HUSHABYE. Pull it and try. Other women can snare men in their hair; but I can swing a baby on mine. Aha! you cant do that, Goldylocks.

ELLIE [*heartbroken*] No. You have stolen my babies.

MRS HUSHABYE. Pettikins: dont make me cry. You know, what you said about my making a household pet of him is a little true. Perhaps he ought to have waited for you. Would any other woman on earth forgive you?

ELLIE. Oh, what right had you to take him all for yourself! [*Pulling herself together*] There! You couldnt help it: neither of us could help it. He couldnt help it. No: dont say anything more: I cant bear it. Let us wake the object. [*She begins stroking Mangan's head, reversing the movement with which she put him to sleep*]. Wake up, do you hear? You are to wake up at once. Wake up, wake up, wake –

MANGAN [*bouncing out of the chair in a fury and turning on them*] Wake up! So you think Ive been asleep, do you? [*He kicks the chair violently out of his way, and gets between them*]. You throw me into a trance so that I cant move hand or foot – I might have been buried alive! it's a mercy I wasnt –

and then you think I was only asleep. If youd let me drop the two times you rolled me about, my nose would have been flattened for life against the floor. But Ive found you all out, anyhow. I know the sort of people I'm among now. Ive heard every word youve said, you and your precious father, and [*to Mrs Hushabye*] you too. So I'm an object, am I? I'm a thing, am I? I'm a fool that hasnt sense enough to feed myself properly, am I? I'm afraid of the men that would starve if it werent for the wages I give them, am I? I'm nothing but a disgusting old skinflint to be made a convenience of by designing women and fool managers of my works, am I? I'm –

MRS HUSHABYE [*with the most elegant aplomb*] Sh-sh-sh-sh-sh! Mr Mangan: you are bound in honor to obliterate from your mind all you heard while you were pretending to be asleep. It was not meant for you to hear.

MANGAN. Pretending to be asleep! Do you think if I was only pretending that I'd have sprawled there helpless, and listened to such unfairness, such lies, such injustice and plotting and backbiting and slandering of me, if I could have up and told you what I thought of you! I wonder I didnt burst.

MRS HUSHABYE [*sweetly*] You dreamt it all, Mr Mangan. We were only saying how beautifully peaceful you looked in your sleep. That was all, wasnt it, Ellie? Believe me, Mr Mangan, all those unpleasant things came into your mind in the last half second before you woke. Ellie rubbed your hair the wrong way; and the disagreeable sensation suggested a disagreeable dream.

MANGAN [*doggedly*] I believe in dreams.

MRS HUSHABYE. So do I. But they go by contraries, dont they?

MANGAN [*depths of emotion suddenly welling up in him*] I shant forget, to my dying day, that when you gave me the glad eye that time in the garden, you were making a fool of me. That was a dirty low mean thing to do. You had no right to let me come near you if I disgusted you. It isnt my fault if I'm old and havnt a moustache like a bronze candlestick as your husband has. There are things no decent woman would do to a man – like a man hitting a woman in the breast.

Hesione, utterly shamed, sits down on the sofa and covers her face with her hands. Mangan sits down also on his chair and begins to cry like a child. Ellie stares at them. Mrs Hushabye, at the distressing sound he makes, takes down her hands and looks at him. She rises and runs to him.

MRS HUSHABYE. Dont cry: I cant bear it. Have I broken your heart? I didnt know you had one. How could I?

MANGAN. I'm a man aint I?

MRS HUSHABYE [*half coaxing, half rallying, altogether tenderly*] Oh no: not what I call a man. Only a Boss: just that and nothing else. What business has a Boss with a heart?

MANGAN. Then youre not a bit sorry for what you did, nor ashamed?

MRS HUSHABYE. I was ashamed for the first time in my life when you said that about hitting a woman in the breast, and I found out what I'd done. My very bones blushed red. Youve had your revenge, Boss. Arnt you satisfied?

MANGAN. Serve you right! Do you hear? Serve you right! Youre just cruel. Cruel.

MRS HUSHABYE. Yes: cruelty would be delicious if one could only find some sort of cruelty that didnt really hurt. By the way [*sitting down beside him on the arm of the chair*], whats your name? It's not really Boss, is it?

MANGAN [*shortly*] If you want to know, my name's Alfred.

MRS HUSHABYE [*springing up*] Alfred!! Ellie: he was christened after Tennyson!!!

MANGAN [*rising*] I was christened after my uncle, and never had a penny from him, damn him! What of it?

MRS HUSHABYE. It comes to me suddenly that you are a

112

real person: that you had a mother, like anyone else. [*Putting her hands on his shoulders and surveying him*] Little Alf!

MANGAN. Well, you have a nerve.

MRS HUSHABYE. And you have a heart, Alfy, a whimpering little heart, but a real one. [*Releasing him suddenly*] Now run and make it up with Ellie. She has had time to think what to say to you, which is more than I had [*she goes out quickly into the garden by the port door*].

MANGAN. That woman has a pair of hands that go right through you.

ELLIE. Still in love with her, in spite of all we said about you?

MANGAN. Are all women like you two? Do they never think of anything about a man except what they can get out of him? You werent even thinking that about me. You were only thinking whether your gloves would last.

ELLIE. I shall not have to think about that when we are married.

MANGAN. And you think I am going to marry you after what I heard there!

ELLIE. You heard nothing from me that I did not tell you before.

MANGAN. Perhaps you think I cant do without you.

ELLIE. I think you would feel lonely without us all now, after coming to know us so well.

MANGAN [*with something like a yell of despair*] Am I never to have the last word?

CAPTAIN SHOTOVER [*appearing at the starboard garden door*] There is a soul in torment here. What is the matter?

MANGAN. This girl doesnt want to spend her life wondering how long her gloves will last.

CAPTAIN SHOTOVER [*passing through*] Dont wear any. I never do [*he goes into the pantry*].

LADY UTTERWORD [*appearing at the port garden door, in a handsome dinner dress*] Is anything the matter?

ELLIE. This gentleman wants to know is he never to have the last word?

LADY UTTERWORD [*coming forward to the sofa*] I should let him have it, my dear. The important thing is not to have the last word, but to have your own way.

MANGAN. She wants both.

LADY UTTERWORD. She wont get them, Mr Mangan. Providence always has the last word.

MANGAN [*desperately*] Now you are going to come religion over me. In this house a man's mind might as well be a football. I'm going. [*He makes for the hall, but is stopped by a hail from the Captain, who has just emerged from his pantry*].

CAPTAIN SHOTOVER. Whither away, Boss Mangan?

MANGAN. To hell out of this house: let that be enough for you and all here.

CAPTAIN SHOTOVER. You were welcome to come: you are free to go. The wide earth, the high seas, the spacious skies are waiting for you outside.

LADY UTTERWORD. But your things, Mr Mangan. Your bags, your comb and brushes, your pyjamas –

HECTOR [*who has just appeared in the port doorway in a handsome Arab costume*] Why should the escaping slave take his chains with him?

MANGAN. Thats right, Hushabye. Keep the pyjamas, my lady; and much good may they do you.

HECTOR [*advancing to Lady Utterword's left hand*] Let us all go out into the night and leave everything behind us.

MANGAN. You stay where you are, the lot of you. I want no company, especially female company.

ELLIE. Let him go. He is unhappy here. He is angry with us.

CAPTAIN SHOTOVER. Go, Boss Mangan; and when you have found the land where there is happiness and where there are no women, send me its latitude and longitude; and I will join you there.

LADY UTTERWORD. You will certainly not be comfortable without your luggage, Mr Mangan.

ELLIE [*impatient*] Go, go: why dont you go? It is a heavenly night: you can sleep on the heath. Take my waterproof to lie on: it is hanging up in the hall.

HECTOR. Breakfast at nine, unless you prefer to breakfast with the Captain at six.

ELLIE. Good night, Alfred.

HECTOR. Alfred! [*He runs back to the door and calls into the garden*] Randall: Mangan's Christian name is Alfred.

RANDALL [*appearing in the starboard doorway in evening dress*] Then Hesione wins her bet.

Mrs Hushabye appears in the port doorway. She throws her left arm round Hector's neck; draws him with her to the back of the sofa; and throws her right arm round Lady Utterword's neck.

MRS HUSHABYE. They wouldnt believe me, Alf.

They contemplate him.

MANGAN. Is there any more of you coming in to look at me, as if I was the latest thing in a menagerie.

MRS HUSHABYE. You are the latest thing in this menagerie.

Before Mangan can retort, a fall of furniture is heard from upstairs; then a pistol shot, and a yell of pain. The staring group breaks up in consternation.

MAZZINI'S VOICE [*from above*] Help! A burglar! Help!

HECTOR [*his eyes blazing*] A burglar!!!

MRS HUSHABYE. No, Hector: youll be shot [*but it is too late: he has dashed out past Mangan, who hastily moves towards the bookshelves out of his way*].

CAPTAIN SHOTOVER [*blowing his whistle*] All hands aloft! [*He strides out after Hector*].

LADY UTTERWORD. My diamonds! [*She follows the Captain*].

RANDALL [*rushing after her*] No, Ariadne. Let me.

ELLIE. Oh, is papa shot? [*she runs out*].

MRS HUSHABYE. Are you frightened, Alf?

MANGAN. No. It aint my house, thank God.

MRS HUSHABYE. If they catch a burglar, shall we have to go into court as witnesses, and be asked all sorts of questions about our private lives?

MANGAN. You wont be believed if you tell the truth.

Mazzini, terribly upset, with a duelling pistol in his hand, comes from the hall, and makes his way to the drawing-table.

MAZZINI. Oh, my dear Mrs Hushabye, I might have killed him [*He throws the pistol on the table and staggers round to the chair*]. I hope you wont believe I really intended to.

Hector comes in, marching an old and villainous looking man before him by the collar. He plants him in the middle of the room and releases him.

Ellie follows, and immediately runs across to the back of her father's chair, and pats his shoulders.

RANDALL [*entering with a poker*] Keep your eye on this door, Mangan. I'll look after the other [*he goes to the starboard door and stands on guard there*].

Lady Utterword comes in after Randall, and goes between Mrs Hushabye and Mangan.

Nurse Guinness brings up the rear, and waits near the door, on Mangan's left.

MRS HUSHABYE. What has happened?

MAZZINI. Your housekeeper told me there was somebody upstairs, and gave me a pistol that Mr Hushabye had been practising with. I thought it would frighten him; but it went off at a touch.

THE BURGLAR. Yes, and took the skin off my ear. Precious near took the top off my head. Why dont you have a proper revolver instead of a thing like that, that goes off if you as much as blow on it?

HECTOR. One of my duelling pistols. Sorry.

MAZZINI. He put his hands up and said it was a fair cop.

THE BURGLAR. So it was. Send for the police.

HECTOR. No, by thunder! It was not a fair cop. We were four to one.

MRS HUSHABYE. What will they do to him?

THE BURGLAR. Ten years. Beginning with solitary. Ten years off my life. I shant serve it all: I'm too old. It will see me out.

LADY UTTERWORD. You should have thought of that before you stole my diamonds.

THE BURGLAR. Well, youve got them back, lady: havnt you? Can you give me back the years of my life you are going to take from me?

MRS HUSHABYE. Oh, we cant bury a man alive for ten years for a few diamonds.

THE BURGLAR. Ten little shining diamonds! Ten long black years!

LADY UTTERWORD. Think of what it is for us to be dragged through the horrors of a criminal court, and have all our family affairs in the papers! If you were a native, and Hastings could order you a good beating and send you away, I shouldnt mind; but here in England there is no real protection for any respectable person.

THE BURGLAR. I'm too old to be giv a hiding, lady. Send for the police and have done with it. It's only just and right you should.

RANDALL [who has relaxed his vigilance on seeing the burglar so pacifically disposed, and comes forward swinging the poker between his fingers like a well-folded umbrella] It is neither just nor right that we should be put to a lot of inconvenience to gratify your moral enthusiasm, my friend. You had better get out, while you have the chance.

THE BURGLAR [inexorably] No. I must work my sin off my conscience. This has come as a sort of call to me. Let me spend the rest of my life repenting in a cell. I shall have my reward above.

MANGAN [exasperated] The very burglars cant behave naturally in this house.

HECTOR. My good sir: you must work out your salvation at

somebody else's expense. Nobody here is going to charge you.

THE BURGLAR. Oh, you wont charge me, wont you?

HECTOR. No. I'm sorry to be inhospitable; but will you kindly leave the house?

THE BURGLAR. Right. I'll go to the police station and give myself up. [*He turns resolutely to the door; but Hector stops him*].

HECTOR. Oh no. You mustnt do that.

RANDALL. No, no. Clear out, man, cant you; and dont be a fool.

MRS HUSHABYE. Dont be so silly. Cant you repent at home?

LADY UTTERWORD. You will have to do as you are told.

THE BURGLAR. It's compounding a felony, you know.

MRS HUSHABYE. This is utterly ridiculous. Are we to be forced to prosecute this man when we dont want to?

THE BURGLAR. Am I to be robbed of my salvation to save you the trouble of spending a day at the sessions? Is that justice? Is it right? Is it fair to me?

MAZZINI [*rising and leaning across the table persuasively as if it were a pulpit desk or a shop counter*] Come, come! let me shew you how you can turn your very crimes to account. Why not set up as a locksmith? You must know more about locks than most honest men?

THE BURGLAR. Thats true, sir. But I couldnt set up as a locksmith under twenty pounds.

RANDALL. Well, you can easily steal twenty pounds. You will find it in the nearest bank.

THE BURGLAR [*horrified*] Oh what a thing for a gentleman to put into the head of a poor criminal scrambling out of the bottomless pit as it were! Oh, shame on you, sir! Oh, God forgive you! [*He throws himself into the big chair and covers his face as if in prayer*].

LADY UTTERWORD. Really, Randall!

HECTOR. It seems to me that we shall have to take up a collection for this inopportunely contrite sinner.

LADY UTTERWORD. But twenty pounds is ridiculous.

THE BURGLAR [*looking up quickly*] I shall have to buy a lot of tools, lady.

LADY UTTERWORD. Nonsense: you have your burgling kit.

THE BURGLAR. Whats a jemmy and a centrebit and an acetylene welding plant and a bunch of skeleton keys? I shall want a forge, and a smithy, and a shop, and fittings. I cant hardly do it for twenty.

HECTOR. My worthy friend, we havnt got twenty pounds.

THE BURGLAR [*now master of the situation*] You can raise it among you, cant you?

MRS HUSHABYE. Give him a sovereign, Hector; and get rid of him.

HECTOR [*giving him a pound*] There! Off with you.

THE BURGLAR [*rising and taking the money very ungratefully*] I wont promise nothing. You have more on you than a quid: all the lot of you, I mean.

LADY UTTERWORD [*vigorously*] Oh, let us prosecute him and have done with it. I have a conscience too, I hope; and I do not feel at all sure that we have any right to let him go, especially if he is going to be greedy and impertinent.

THE BURGLAR [*quickly*] All right, lady, all right. I've no wish to be anything but agreeable. Good evening, ladies and gentlemen; and thank you kindly.

He is hurrying out when he is confronted in the doorway by Captain Shotover.

CAPTAIN SHOTOVER [*fixing the burglar with a piercing regard*] What's this? Are there two of you?

THE BURGLAR [*falling on his knees before the Captain in abject terror*] Oh my good Lord, what have I done? Dont tell me it's your house Ive broken into, Captain Shotover.

The Captain seizes him by the collar; drags him to his feet; and leads him to the middle of the group, Hector falling back beside his wife to make way for them.

CAPTAIN SHOTOVER [*turning him towards Ellie*] Is that your daughter? [*He releases him*].

THE BURGLAR. Well, how do I know, Captain? You know the sort of life you and me has led. Any young lady of that age might be my daughter anywhere in the wide world, as you might say.

CAPTAIN SHOTOVER [*to Mazzini*] You are not Billy Dunn. This is Billy Dunn. Why have you imposed on me?

THE BURGLAR [*indignantly to Mazzini*] Have you been giving yourself out to be me? You, that nigh blew my head off! Shooting yourself, in a manner of speaking!

MAZZINI. My dear Captain Shotover, ever since I came into this house I have done hardly anything else but assure you that I am not Mr William Dunn, but Mazzini Dunn, a very different person.

THE BURGLAR. He dont belong to my branch, Captain. Theres two sets in the family: the thinking Dunns and the drinking Dunns, each going their own ways. I'm a drinking Dunn: he's a thinking Dunn. But that didnt give him any right to shoot me.

CAPTAIN SHOTOVER. So youve turned burglar, have you?

THE BURGLAR. No, Captain: I wouldnt disgrace our old sea calling by such a thing. I am no burglar.

LADY UTTERWORD. What were you doing with my diamonds?

GUINNESS. What did you break into the house for if youre no burglar?

RANDALL. Mistook the house for your own and came in by the wrong window, eh?

THE BURGLAR. Well, it's no use my telling you a lie: I can take in most captains, but not Captain Shotover, because he sold himself to the devil in Zanzibar, and can divine water, spot gold, explode a cartridge in your pocket with a glance of his eye, and see the truth hidden in the heart of man. But I'm no burglar.

CAPTAIN SHOTOVER. Are you an honest man?

THE BURGLAR. I dont set up to be better than my fellow-creatures, and never did, as you well know, Captain. But what I do is innocent and pious. I enquire about for houses where the right sort of people live. I work it on them same as I worked it here. I break into the house; put a few spoons or diamonds in my pocket; make a noise; get caught; and take up a collection. And you wouldnt believe how hard it is to get caught when youre actually trying to. I have knocked over all the chairs in a room without a soul paying any attention to me. In the end I have had to walk out and leave the job.

RANDALL. When that happens, do you put back the spoons and diamonds?

THE BURGLAR. Well, I dont fly in the face of Providence, if thats what you want to know.

CAPTAIN SHOTOVER. Guinness: you remember this man?

GUINNESS. I should think I do, seeing I was married to him, the blackguard!

HESIONE ⎱ *exclaiming* ⎰ Married to him!
LADY UTTERWORD ⎰ *together* ⎱ Guinness!!

THE BURGLAR. It wasnt legal. Ive been married to no end of women. No use coming that over me.

CAPTAIN SHOTOVER. Take him to the forecastle [*he flings him to the door with a strength beyond his years*].

GUINNESS. I suppose you mean the kitchen. They wont have him there. Do you expect servants to keep company with thieves and all sorts?

CAPTAIN SHOTOVER. Land-thieves and water-thieves are the same flesh and blood. I'll have no boatswain on my quarter-deck. Off with you both.

THE BURGLAR. Yes, Captain. [*He goes out humbly*].

MAZZINI. Will it be safe to have him in the house like that?

GUINNESS. Why didnt you shoot him, sir? If I'd known who he was, I'd have shot him myself. [*She goes out*].

MRS HUSHABYE. Do sit down, everybody. [*She sits down on the sofa*].

They all move except Ellie. Mazzini resumes his seat. Randall sits down in the window seat near the starboard door, again making a pendulum of his poker, and studying it as Galileo might have done. Hector sits on his left, in the middle. Mangan, forgotten, sits in the port corner. Lady Utterword takes the big chair. Captain Shotover goes into the pantry in deep abstraction. They all look after him; and Lady Utterword coughs unconsciously.

MRS HUSHABYE. So Billy Dunn was poor nurse's little romance. I knew there had been somebody.

RANDALL. They will fight their battles over again and enjoy themselves immensely.

LADY UTTERWORD [*irritably*] You are not married; and you know nothing about it, Randall. Hold your tongue.

RANDALL. Tyrant!

MRS HUSHABYE. Well, we have had a very exciting evening. Everything will be an anticlimax after it. We'd better all go to bed.

RANDALL. Another burglar may turn up.

MAZZINI. Oh, impossible! I hope not.

RANDALL. Why not? There is more than one burglar in England.

MRS HUSHABYE. What do you say, Alf?

MANGAN [*huffily*] Oh, I dont matter. I'm forgotten. The burglar has put my nose out of joint. Shove me into a corner and have done with me.

MRS HUSHABYE [*jumping up mischievously, and going to him*] Would you like a walk on the heath, Alfred? With me?

ELLIE. Go, Mr Mangan. It will do you good. Hesione will soothe you.

MRS HUSHABYE [*slipping her arm under his and pulling him up-*

right] Come, Alfred. There is a moon: it's like the night in Tristan and Isolde. [*She caresses his arm and draws him to the port garden door*].

MANGAN [*writhing but yielding*] How you can have the face – the heart – [*he breaks down and is heard sobbing as she takes him out.*]

LADY UTTERWORD. What an extraordinary way to behave! What is the matter with the man?

ELLIE [*in a strangely calm voice, staring into an imaginary distance*] His heart is breaking: that is all. [*The Captain appears at the pantry door, listening*]. It is a curious sensation: the sort of pain that goes mercifully beyond our powers of feeling. When your heart is broken, your boats are burned: nothing matters any more. It is the end of happiness and the beginning of peace.

LADY UTTERWORD [*suddenly rising in a rage, to the astonishment of the rest*] How dare you?

HECTOR. Good heavens! Whats the matter?

RANDALL [*in a warning whisper*] Tch – tch – tch! Steady.

ELLIE [*surprised and haughty*] I was not addressing you particularly, Lady Utterword. And I am not accustomed to be asked how dare I.

LADY UTTERWORD. Of course not. Anyone can see how badly you have been brought up.

MAZZINI. Oh, I hope not, Lady Utterword. Really!

LADY UTTERWORD. I know very well what you meant. The impudence!

ELLIE. What on earth do you mean?

CAPTAIN SHOTOVER [*advancing to the table*] She means that her heart will not break. She has been longing all her life for someone to break it. At last she has become afraid she has none to break.

LADY UTTERWORD [*flinging herself on her knees and throwing her arms round him*] Papa: dont say you think Ive no heart.

CAPTAIN SHOTOVER [*raising her with grim tenderness*] If you had no heart how could you want to have it broken, child?

HECTOR [*rising with a bound*] Lady Utterword: you are not to be trusted. You have made a scene [*he runs out into the garden through the starboard door*].

LADY UTTERWORD. Oh! Hector, Hector! [*she runs out after him*].

RANDALL. Only nerves, I assure you. [*He rises and follows her, waving the poker in his agitation*] Ariadne! Ariadne! For God's sake be careful. You will – [*he is gone*].

MAZZINI [*rising*] How distressing! Can I do anything, I wonder?

CAPTAIN SHOTOVER [*promptly taking his chair and setting to work at the drawing-board*] No. Go to bed. Goodnight.

MAZZINI [*bewildered*] Oh! Perhaps you are right.

ELLIE. Goodnight, dearest. [*She kisses him*].

MAZZINI. Goodnight, love. [*He makes for the door, but turns aside to the bookshelves*]. I'll just take a book [*he takes one*]. Goodnight. [*He goes out, leaving Ellie alone with the Captain*].

The Captain is intent on his drawing. Ellie, standing sentry over his chair, contemplates him for a moment.

ELLIE. Does nothing ever disturb you, Captain Shotover?

CAPTAIN SHOTOVER. Ive stood on the bridge for eighteen hours in a typhoon. Life here is stormier; but I can stand it.

ELLIE. Do you think I ought to marry Mr Mangan?

CAPTAIN SHOTOVER [*never looking up*] One rock is as good as another to be wrecked on.

ELLIE. I am not in love with him.

CAPTAIN SHOTOVER. Who said you were?

ELLIE. You are not surprised?

CAPTAIN SHOTOVER. Surprised! At my age!

ELLIE. It seems to me quite fair. He wants me for one thing: I want him for another.

CAPTAIN SHOTOVER. Money?

ELLIE. Yes.

CAPTAIN SHOTOVER. Well, one turns the cheek: the other kisses it. One provides the cash: the other spends it.

ELLIE. Who will have the best of the bargain, I wonder?

CAPTAIN SHOTOVER. You. These fellows live in an office all day. You will have to put up with him from dinner to breakfast; but you will both be asleep most of that time. All day you will be quit of him; and you will be shopping with his money. If that is too much for you, marry a sea-faring man: you will be bothered with him only three weeks in the year, perhaps.

ELLIE. That would be best of all, I suppose.

CAPTAIN SHOTOVER. It's a dangerous thing to be married right up to the hilt, like my daughter's husband. The man is at home all day, like a damned soul in hell.

ELLIE. I never thought of that before.

CAPTAIN SHOTOVER. If youre marrying for business, you cant be too businesslike.

ELLIE. Why do women always want other women's husbands?

CAPTAIN SHOTOVER. Why do horse-thieves prefer a horse that is broken-in to one that is wild?

ELLIE [with a short laugh] I suppose so. What a vile world it is!

CAPTAIN SHOTOVER. It doesnt concern me. I'm nearly out of it.

ELLIE. And I'm only just beginning.

CAPTAIN SHOTOVER. Yes; so look ahead.

ELLIE. Well, I think I am being very prudent.

CAPTAIN SHOTOVER. I didnt say prudent. I said look ahead.

ELLIE. Whats the difference?

CAPTAIN SHOTOVER. It's prudent to gain the whole world and lose your own soul. But dont forget that your soul sticks to you if you stick to it; but the world has a way of slipping through your fingers.

ELLIE [*wearily, leaving him and beginning to wander restlessly about the room*] I'm sorry, Captain Shotover; but it's no use talking like that to me. Old-fashioned people are no use to me. Old-fashioned people think you can have a soul without money. They think the less money you have, the more soul you have. Young people nowadays know better. A soul is a very expensive thing to keep: much more so than a motor car.

CAPTAIN SHOTOVER. Is it? How much does your soul eat?

ELLIE. Oh, a lot. It eats music and pictures and books and mountains and lakes and beautiful things to wear and nice people to be with. In this country you cant have them without lots of money: that is why our souls are so horribly starved.

CAPTAIN SHOTOVER. Mangan's soul lives on pigs' food.

ELLIE. Yes: money is thrown away on him. I suppose his soul was starved when he was young. But it will not be thrown away on me. It is just because I want to save my soul that I am marrying for money. All the women who are not fools do.

CAPTAIN SHOTOVER. There are other ways of getting money. Why dont you steal it?

ELLIE. Because I dont want to go to prison.

CAPTAIN SHOTOVER. Is that the only reason? Are you quite sure honesty has nothing to do with it?

ELLIE. Oh, you are very very old-fashioned, Captain. Does any modern girl believe that the legal and illegal ways of getting money are the honest and dishonest ways? Mangan robbed my father and my father's friends. I should rob all the money back from Mangan if the police would let me. As they wont, I must get it back by marrying him.

CAPTAIN SHOTOVER. I cant argue: I'm too old: my mind is made up and finished. All I can tell you is that, old-fashioned or new-fashioned, if you sell yourself, you deal your soul a blow that all the books and pictures and concerts and scenery in the world wont heal [*he gets up suddenly and makes for the pantry*].

ELLIE [*running after him and seizing him by the sleeve*] Then why did you sell yourself to the devil in Zanzibar?

CAPTAIN SHOTOVER [*stopping, startled*] What?

ELLIE. You shall not run away before you answer. I have found out that trick of yours. If you sold yourself, why shouldnt I?

CAPTAIN SHOTOVER. I had to deal with men so degraded that they wouldnt obey me unless I swore at them and kicked them and beat them with my fists. Foolish people took young thieves off the streets; flung them into a training ship where they were taught to fear the cane instead of fearing God; and thought theyd made men and sailors of them by private subscription. I tricked these thieves into believing I'd sold myself to the devil. It saved my soul from the kicking and swearing that was damning me by inches.

ELLIE [*releasing him*] I shall pretend to sell myself to Boss Mangan to save my soul from the poverty that is damning me by inches.

CAPTAIN SHOTOVER. Riches will damn you ten times deeper. Riches wont save even your body.

ELLIE. Old-fashioned again. We know now that the soul is the body, and the body the soul. They tell us they are different because they want to persuade us that we can keep our souls if we let them make slaves of our bodies. I am afraid you are no use to me, Captain.

CAPTAIN SHOTOVER. What did you expect? A Savior, eh? Are you old-fashioned enough to believe in that?

ELLIE. No. But I thought you were very wise, and might help me. Now I have found you out. You pretend to be busy, and think of fine things to say, and run in and out to surprise people by saying them, and get away before they can answer you.

CAPTAIN SHOTOVER. It confuses me to be answered. It discourages me. I cannot bear men and women. I have to run away. I must run away now [*he tries to*].

ELLIE [*again seizing his arm*] You shall not run away from me. I can hypnotize you. You are the only person in the house I can say what I like to. I know you are fond of me. Sit down. [*She draws him to the sofa*].

CAPTAIN SHOTOVER [*yielding*] Take care: I am in my dotage. Old men are dangerous: it doesnt matter to them what is going to happen to the world.

They sit side by side on the sofa. She leans affectionately against him with her head on his shoulder and her eyes half closed.

ELLIE [*dreamily*] I should have thought nothing else mattered to old men. They cant be very interested in what is going to happen to themselves.

CAPTAIN SHOTOVER. A man's interest in the world is only the overflow from his interest in himself. When you are a child your vessel is not yet full; so you care for nothing but your own affairs. When you grow up, your vessel overflows; and you are a politician, a philosopher, or an explorer and adventurer. In old age the vessel dries up: there is no overflow: you are a child again. I can give you the memories of my ancient wisdom: mere scraps and leavings; but I no longer really care for anything but my own little wants and hobbies. I sit here working out my old ideas as a means of destroying my fellow-creatures. I see my daughters and their men living foolish lives of romance and sentiment and snobbery. I see you, the younger generation, turning from their romance and sentiment and snobbery to money and comfort and hard common sense. I was ten times happier on the bridge in the typhoon, or frozen into Arctic ice for months in darkness, than you or they have ever been. You are looking for a rich husband. At your age I looked for hardship, danger, horror, and death, that I might feel the life in me more intensely. I did not let the fear of death govern my life; and my reward was, I had my life. You are going to let the fear of poverty govern your life; and your reward will be that you will eat, but you will not live.

ELLIE [*sitting up impatiently*] But what can I do? I am not a sea captain: I cant stand on bridges in typhoons, or go slaughtering seals and whales in Greenland's icy mountains. They wont let women be captains. Do you want me to be a stewardess?

CAPTAIN SHOTOVER. There are worse lives. The stewardesses could come ashore if they liked; but they sail and sail and sail.

ELLIE. What could they do ashore but marry for money? I dont want to be a stewardess: I am too bad a sailor. Think of something else for me.

CAPTAIN SHOTOVER. I cant think so long and continuously. I am too old. I must go in and out. [*He tries to rise*].

ELLIE [*pulling him back*] You shall not. You are happy here, arnt you?

CAPTAIN SHOTOVER. I tell you it's dangerous to keep me. I cant keep awake and alert.

ELLIE. What do you run away for? To sleep?

CAPTAIN SHOTOVER. No. To get a glass of rum.

ELLIE [*frightfully disillusioned*] Is that it? How disgusting! Do you like being drunk?

CAPTAIN SHOTOVER. No: I dread being drunk more than anything in the world. To be drunk means to have dreams; to go soft; to be easily pleased and deceived; to fall into the clutches of women. Drink does that for you when you are young. But when you are old: very very old, like me, the dreams come by themselves. You dont know how terrible that is: you are young: you sleep at night only, and sleep soundly. But later on you will sleep in the afternoon. Later still you will sleep even in the morning; and you will awake tired, tired of life. You will never be free from dozing and dreams: the dreams will steal upon your work every ten minutes unless you can awaken yourself with rum. I drink now to keep sober; but the dreams are conquering: rum is not what it was: I have had ten glasses since you came; and it might be so much water. Go get me another: Guinness knows where it is. You had better see for yourself the horror of an old man drinking.

ELLIE. You shall not drink. Dream. I like you to dream. You must never be in the real world when we talk together.

CAPTAIN SHOTOVER. I am too weary to resist or too weak. I am in my second childhood. I do not see you as you really are. I cant remember what I really am. I feel nothing but the accursed happiness I have dreaded all my life long: the happiness that comes as life goes, the happiness of yielding and dreaming instead of resisting and doing, the sweetness of the fruit that is going rotten.

ELLIE. You dread it almost as much as I used to dread losing my dreams and having to fight and do things. But that is all over for me: my dreams are dashed to pieces. I should like to marry a very old, very rich man. I should like to marry you. I had much rather marry you than marry Mangan. Are you very rich?

CAPTAIN SHOTOVER. No. Living from hand to mouth. And I have a wife somewhere in Jamaica: a black one. My first wife. Unless she's dead.

ELLIE. What a pity! I feel so happy with you. [*She takes his hand, almost unconsciously, and pats it*]. I thought I should never feel happy again.

CAPTAIN SHOTOVER. Why?

ELLIE. Dont you know?

CAPTAIN SHOTOVER. No.

ELLIE. Heartbreak. I fell in love with Hector, and didnt know he was married.

CAPTAIN SHOTOVER. Heartbreak? Are you one of those

who are so sufficient to themselves that they are only happy when they are stripped of everything, even of hope?

ELLIE [*gripping the hand*] It seems so; for I feel now as if there was nothing I could not do, because I want nothing.

CAPTAIN SHOTOVER. Thats the only real strength. Thats genius. Thats better than rum.

ELLIE [*throwing away his hand*] Rum! Why did you spoil it?

Hector and Randall come in from the garden through the starboard door.

HECTOR. I beg your pardon. We did not know there was anyone here.

ELLIE [*rising*] That means that you want to tell Mr Randall the story about the tiger. Come, Captain: I want to talk to my father; and you had better come with me.

CAPTAIN SHOTOVER [*rising*] Nonsense! the man is in bed.

ELLIE. Aha! Ive caught you. My real father has gone to bed; but the father you gave me is in the kitchen. You knew quite well all along. Come. [*She draws him out into the garden with her through the port door*].

HECTOR. Thats an extraordinary girl. She has the Ancient Mariner on a string like a Pekinese dog.

RANDALL. Now that they have gone, shall we have a friendly chat?

HECTOR. You are in what is supposed to be my house. I am at your disposal.

Hector sits down in the draughtsman's chair, turning it to face Randall, who remains standing, leaning at his ease against the carpenter's bench.

RANDALL. I take it that we may be quite frank. I mean about Lady Utterword.

HECTOR. You may. I have nothing to be frank about. I never met her until this afternoon.

RANDALL [*straightening up*] What! But you are her sister's husband.

HECTOR. Well, if you come to that, you are her husband's brother.

RANDALL. But you seem to be on intimate terms with her.

HECTOR. So do you.

RANDALL. Yes; but I am on intimate terms with her. I have known her for years.

HECTOR. It took her years to get to the same point with you that she got to with me in five minutes, it seems.

RANDALL [*vexed*] Really, Ariadne is the limit [*he moves away huffishly towards the windows*].

HECTOR [*coolly*] She is, as I remarked to Hesione, a very enterprising woman.

RANDALL [*returning, much troubled*] You see, Hushabye, you are what women consider a good-looking man.

HECTOR. I cultivated that appearance in the days of my vanity; and Hesione insists on my keeping it up. She makes me wear these ridiculous things [*indicating his Arab costume*] because she thinks me absurd in evening dress.

RANDALL. Still, you do keep it up, old chap. Now, I assure you I have not an atom of jealousy in my disposition –

HECTOR. The question would seem to be rather whether your brother has any touch of that sort.

RANDALL. What! Hastings! Oh, dont trouble about Hastings. He has the gift of being able to work sixteen hours a day at the dullest detail, and actually likes it. That gets him to the top wherever he goes. As long as Ariadne takes care that he is fed regularly, he is only too thankful to anyone who will keep her in good humor for him.

HECTOR. And as she has all the Shotover fascination, there is plenty of competition for the job, eh?

RANDALL [*angrily*] She encourages them. Her conduct is perfectly scandalous. I assure you, my dear fellow, I havnt an atom of jealousy in my composition; but she makes herself the talk of every place she goes to by her thoughtlessness. It's nothing more: she doesnt really care for the men she keeps hanging about her; but how is the world to know that? It's not fair to Hastings. It's not fair to me.

HECTOR. Her theory is that her conduct is so correct –

RANDALL. Correct! She does nothing but make scenes from morning til night. You be careful, old chap. She will get you into trouble: that is, she would if she really cared for you.

HECTOR. Doesnt she?

RANDALL. Not a scrap. She may want your scalp to add to her collection; but her true affection has been engaged years ago. You had really better be careful.

HECTOR. Do you suffer much from this jealousy?

RANDALL. Jealousy! I jealous! My dear fellow, havnt I told you that there is not an atom of –

HECTOR. Yes. And Lady Utterword told me she never made scenes. Well, dont waste your jealousy on my moustache. Never waste jealousy on a real man: it is the imaginary hero that supplants us all in the long run. Besides, jealousy does not belong to your easy man-of-the-world pose, which you carry so well in other respects.

RANDALL. Really, Hushabye, I think a man may be allowed to be a gentleman without being accused of posing.

HECTOR. It is a pose like any other. In this house we know all the poses: our game is to find out the man under the pose. The man under your pose is apparently Ellie's favorite, Othello.

RANDALL. Some of the games in this house are damned annoying, let me tell you.

HECTOR. Yes: I have been their victim for many years. I used to writhe under them at first; but I became accustomed to them. At last I learned to play them.

RANDALL. If it's all the same to you, I had rather you didnt play them on me. You evidently dont quite understand my character, or my notions of good form.

HECTOR. Is it your notion of good form to give away Lady Utterword?

RANDALL [*a childishly plaintive note breaking into his huff*] I have not said a word against Lady Utterword. This is just the conspiracy over again.

HECTOR. What conspiracy?

RANDALL. You know very well, sir. A conspiracy to make me out to be pettish and jealous and childish and everything I am not. Everyone knows I am just the opposite.

HECTOR [*rising*] Something in the air of the house has upset you. It often does have that effect. [*He goes to the garden door and calls Lady Utterword with commanding emphasis*] Ariadne!

LADY UTTERWORD [*at some distance*] Yes.

RANDALL. What are you calling her for? I want to speak –

LADY UTTERWORD [*arriving breathless*] Yes. You really are a terribly commanding person. Whats the matter?

HECTOR. I do not know how to manage your friend Randall. No doubt you do.

LADY UTTERWORD. Randall: have you been making yourself ridiculous, as usual? I can see it in your face. Really, you are the most pettish creature.

RANDALL. You know quite well, Ariadne, that I have not an ounce of pettishness in my disposition. I have made myself perfectly pleasant here. I have remained absolutely cool and imperturbable in the face of a burglar. Imperturbability is almost too strong a point of mine. But [*putting his foot down with a stamp, and walking angrily up and down the room*] I insist on being treated with a certain consideration. I will not allow Hushabye to take liberties with me. I will not stand your encouraging people as you do.

HECTOR. The man has a rooted delusion that he is your husband.

LADY UTTERWORD. I know. He is jealous. As if he had any right to be! He compromises me everywhere. He makes scenes all over the place. Randall: I will not allow it. I simply will not allow it. You had no right to discuss me with Hector. I will not be discussed by men.

HECTOR. Be reasonable, Ariadne. Your fatal gift of beauty forces men to discuss you.

LADY UTTERWORD. Oh indeed! what about your fatal gift of beauty?

HECTOR. How can I help it?

LADY UTTERWORD. You could cut off your moustache: I cant cut off my nose. I get my whole life messed up with people falling in love with me. And then Randall says I run after men.

RANDALL. I —

LADY UTTERWORD. Yes you do: you said it just now. Why cant you think of something else than women? Napoleon was quite right when he said that women are the occupation of the idle man. Well, if ever there was an idle man on earth, his name is Randall Utterword.

RANDALL. Ariad —

LADY UTTERWORD [*overwhelming him with a torrent of words*] Oh yes you are: it's no use denying it. What have you ever done? What good are you? You are as much trouble in the house as a child of three. You couldnt live without your valet.

RANDALL. This is —

LADY UTTERWORD. Laziness! You are laziness incarnate. You are selfishness itself. You are the most uninteresting man on earth. You cant even gossip about anything but yourself and your grievances and your ailments and the people who have offended you. [*Turning to Hector*] Do you know what they call him, Hector?

HECTOR.   ] [*speaking* (Please dont tell me.
RANDALL. | *together*] (I'll not stand it —

LADY UTTERWORD. Randall the Rotter: that is his name in good society.

RANDALL [*shouting*] I'll not bear it, I tell you. Will you listen to me, you infernal – [*he chokes*].

LADY UTTERWORD. Well: go on. What were you going to call me? An infernal what? Which unpleasant animal is it to be this time?

RANDALL [*foaming*] There is no animal in the world so hateful as a woman can be. You are a maddening devil. Hushabye: you will not believe me when I tell you that I have loved this demon all my life; but God knows I have paid for it [*he sits down in the draughtsman's chair, weeping*].

LADY UTTERWORD [*standing over him with triumphant contempt*] Cry-baby!

HECTOR [*gravely, coming to him*] My friend: the Shotover sisters have two strange powers over men. They can make them love; and they can make them cry. Thank your stars that you are not married to one of them.

LADY UTTERWORD [*haughtily*] And pray, Hector –

HECTOR [*suddenly catching her round the shoulders; swinging her right round him and away from Randall; and gripping her throat with the other hand*] Ariadne: if you attempt to start on me, I'll choke you: do you hear? The cat-and-mouse game with the other sex is a good game; but I can play your head off at it. [*He throws her, not at all gently, into the big chair, and proceeds, less fiercely but firmly*] It is true that Napoleon said that woman is the occupation of the idle man. But he added that she is the relaxation of the warrior. Well, *I* am the warrior. So take care.

LADY UTTERWORD [*not in the least put out, and rather pleased by his violence*] My dear Hector: I have only done what you asked me to do.

HECTOR. How do you make that out, pray?

LADY UTTERWORD. You called me in to manage Randall, didnt you? You said you couldnt manage him yourself.

HECTOR. Well, what if I did? I did not ask you to drive the man mad.

LADY UTTERWORD. He isnt mad. Thats the way to manage him. If you were a mother, youd understand.

HECTOR. Mother! What are you up to now?

LADY UTTERWORD. It's quite simple. When the children got nerves and were naughty, I smacked them just enough to give them a good cry and a healthy nervous shock. They went to sleep and were quite good afterwards. Well, I cant smack Randall: he is too big; so when he gets nerves and is naughty, I just rag him till he cries. He will be all right now. Look: he is half asleep already [*which is quite true*].

RANDALL [*waking up indignantly*] I'm not. You are most cruel, Ariadne. [*Sentimentally*] But I suppose I must forgive you, as usual [*he checks himself in the act of yawning*].

LADY UTTERWORD [*to Hector*] Is the explanation satisfactory, dread warrior?

HECTOR. Some day I shall kill you, if you go too far. I thought you were a fool.

LADY UTTERWORD [*laughing*] Everybody does, at first. But I am not such a fool as I look. [*She rises complacently*]. Now, Randall: go to bed. You will be a good boy in the morning.

RANDALL [*only very faintly rebellious*] I'll go to bed when I like. It isnt ten yet.

LADY UTTERWORD. It is long past ten. See that he goes to bed at once, Hector. [*She goes into the garden*].

HECTOR. Is there any slavery on earth viler than this slavery of men to women?

RANDALL [*rising resolutely*] I'll not speak to her tomorrow. I'll not speak to her for another week. I'll give her such a lesson. I'll go straight to bed without bidding her goodnight. [*He makes for the door leading to the hall*].

HECTOR. You are under a spell, man. Old Shotover sold himself to the devil in Zanzibar. The devil gave him a black witch for a wife; and these two demon daughters are their mystical progeny. I am tied to Hesione's apronstring; but I'm her husband; and if I did go stark staring mad about her, at least we became man and wife. But why should you let yourself be dragged about and beaten by Ariadne as a toy donkey is dragged about and beaten by a child? What do you get by it? Are you her lover?

RANDALL. You must not misunderstand me. In a higher sense – in a Platonic sense –

HECTOR. Psha! Platonic sense! She makes you her servant; and when pay-day comes round, she bilks you: that is what you mean.

RANDALL [*feebly*] Well, if I dont mind, I dont see what business it is of yours. Besides, I tell you I am going to punish her. You shall see: *I* know how to deal with women. I'm really very sleepy. Say goodnight to Mrs Hushabye for me, will you, like a good chap. Goodnight. [*He hurries out*].

HECTOR. Poor wretch! Oh women! women! women! [*He lifts his fists in invocation to heaven*] Fall. Fall and crush. [*He goes out into the garden*].

ACT III

In the garden, Hector, as he comes out through the glass door of the poop, finds Lady Utterword lying voluptuously in the hammock on the east side of the flagstaff, in the circle of light cast by the electric arc, which is like a moon in its opal globe. Beneath the head of the hammock, a campstool. On the other side of the flagstaff, on the long garden seat, Captain Shotover is asleep, with Ellie beside him, leaning affectionately against him on his right hand. On his left is a deck chair. Behind them in the gloom, Hesione is strolling about with Mangan. It is a fine still night, moonless.

LADY UTTERWORD. What a lovely night! It seems made for us.

HECTOR. The night takes no interest in us. What are we to the night? [*He sits down moodily in the deck chair*].

ELLIE [*dreamily, nestling against the Captain*] Its beauty soaks into my nerves. In the night there is peace for the old and hope for the young.

HECTOR. Is that remark your own?

ELLIE. No. Only the last thing the Captain said before he went to sleep.

CAPTAIN SHOTOVER. I'm not asleep.

HECTOR. Randall is. Also Mr Mazzini Dunn. Mangan too, probably.

MANGAN. No.

HECTOR. Oh, you are there. I thought Hesione would have sent you to bed by this time.

MRS HUSHABYE [*coming to the back of the garden seat, into the light, with Mangan*] I think I shall. He keeps telling me he has a presentiment that he is going to die. I never met a man so greedy for sympathy.

MANGAN [*plaintively*] But I have a presentiment. I really have. And you wouldnt listen.

MRS HUSHABYE. I was listening for something else. There was a sort of splendid drumming in the sky. Did none of you hear it? It came from a distance and then died away.

MANGAN. I tell you it was a train.

MRS HUSHABYE. And *I* tell you, Alf, there is no train at this hour. The last is nine fortyfive.

MANGAN. But a goods train.

MRS HUSHABYE. Not on our little line. They tack a truck on to the passenger train. What can it have been, Hector?

HECTOR. Heaven's threatening growl of disgust at us useless futile creatures. [*Fiercely*] I tell you, one of two things must happen. Either out of that darkness some new creation will come to supplant us as we have supplanted the animals, or the heavens will fall in thunder and destroy us.

LADY UTTERWORD [*in a cool instructive manner, wallowing comfortably in her hammock*] We have not supplanted the animals, Hector. Why do you ask heaven to destroy this house, which could be made quite comfortable if Hesione had any notion of how to live? Dont you know what is wrong with it?

HECTOR. We are wrong with it. There is no sense in us. We are useless, dangerous, and ought to be abolished.

LADY UTTERWORD. Nonsense! Hastings told me the very first day he came here, nearly twentyfour years ago, what is wrong with the house.

CAPTAIN SHOTOVER. What! The numskull said there was something wrong with my house!

LADY UTTERWORD. I said Hastings said it; and he is not in the least a numskull.

CAPTAIN SHOTOVER. Whats wrong with my house?

LADY UTTERWORD. Just what is wrong with a ship, papa. Wasnt it clever of Hastings to see that?

CAPTAIN SHOTOVER. The man's a fool. Theres nothing wrong with a ship.

LADY UTTERWORD. Yes there is.

MRS HUSHABYE. But what is it? Dont be aggravating, Addy.

LADY UTTERWORD. Guess.

HECTOR. Demons. Daughters of the witch of Zanzibar. Demons.

LADY UTTERWORD. Not a bit. I assure you, all this house needs to make it a sensible, healthy, pleasant house, with good appetites and sound sleep in it, is horses.

MRS HUSHABYE. Horses! What rubbish!

LADY UTTERWORD. Yes: horses. Why have we never been able to let this house? Because there are no proper stables. Go anywhere in England where there are natural, wholesome, contented, and really nice English people; and what do you always find? That the stables are the real centre of the household; and that if any visitor wants to play the piano the whole room has to be upset before it can be opened, there are so many things piled on it. I never lived until I learned to ride; and I shall never ride really well because I didnt begin as a child. There are only two classes in good society in England: the equestrian classes and the neurotic classes. It isnt mere convention: everybody can see that the people who hunt are the right people and the people who dont are the wrong ones.

CAPTAIN SHOTOVER. There is some truth in this. My ship made a man of me; and a ship is the horse of the sea.

LADY UTTERWORD. Exactly how Hastings explained your being a gentleman.

CAPTAIN SHOTOVER. Not bad for a numskull. Bring the man here with you next time: I must talk to him.

LADY UTTERWORD. Why is Randall such an obvious rotter? He is well bred; he has been at a public school and a university; he has been in the Foreign Office; he knows the best people and has lived all his life among them. Why is he so unsatisfactory, so contemptible? Why cant he get a valet to stay with him longer than a few months? Just because he is too lazy and pleasure-loving to hunt and shoot. He strums the piano, and sketches, and runs after married women, and reads literary books and poems. He actually plays the flute; but I never let him bring it into my house. If he would only – [*she is interrupted by the melancholy strains of a flute coming from an open window above. She raises herself indignantly in the hammock*]. Randall: you have not gone to bed. Have you been listening? [*The flute replies pertly:*]

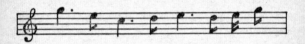

How vulgar! Go to bed instantly, Randall: how dare you? [*The window is slammed down. She subsides*]. How can anyone care for such a creature!

MRS HUSHABYE. Addy: do you think Ellie ought to marry poor Alfred merely for his money?

MANGAN [*much alarmed*] Whats that? Mrs Hushabye: are my affairs to be discussed like this before everybody?

LADY UTTERWORD. I dont think Randall is listening now.

MANGAN. Everybody is listening. It isnt right.

MRS HUSHABYE. But in the dark, what does it matter? Ellie doesnt mind. Do you, Ellie?

ELLIE. Not in the least. What is your opinion, Lady Utterword? You have so much good sense.

MANGAN. But it isnt right. It – [*Mrs Hushabye puts her hand on his mouth*]. Oh, very well.

LADY UTTERWORD. How much money have you, Mr Mangan?

MANGAN. Really – No: I cant stand this.

LADY UTTERWORD. Nonsense, Mr Mangan! It all turns on your income, doesnt it?

MANGAN. Well, if you come to that, how much money has she?

ELLIE. None.

LADY UTTERWORD. You are answered, Mr Mangan. And now, as you have made Miss Dunn throw her cards on the table, you cannot refuse to shew your own.

MRS HUSHABYE. Come, Alf! out with it! How much?

MANGAN [*baited out of all prudence*] Well, if you want to know, I have no money and never had any.

MRS HUSHABYE. Alfred: you mustnt tell naughty stories.

MANGAN. I'm not telling you stories. I'm telling you the raw truth.

LADY UTTERWORD. Then what do you live on, Mr Mangan?

MANGAN. Travelling expenses. And a trifle of commission.

CAPTAIN SHOTOVER. What more have any of us but travelling expenses for our life's journey?

MRS HUSHABYE. But you have factories and capital and things?

MANGAN. People think I have. People think I'm an industrial Napoleon. Thats why Miss Ellie wants to marry me. But I tell you I have nothing.

ELLIE. Do you mean that the factories are like Marcus's tigers? That they dont exist?

MANGAN. They exist all right enough. But theyre not mine. They belong to syndicates and shareholders and all sorts of lazy good-for-nothing capitalists. I get money from such people to start the factories. I find people like Miss Dunn's father to work them, and keep a tight hand so as to make them pay. Of course I make them keep me going pretty well; but it's a dog's life; and I dont own anything.

MRS HUSHABYE. Alfred, Alfred: you are making a poor mouth of it to get out of marrying Ellie.

MANGAN. I'm telling the truth about my money for the first time in my life; and it's the first time my word has ever been doubted.

LADY UTTERWORD. How sad! Why dont you go in for politics, Mr Mangan?

MANGAN. Go in for politics! Where have you been living? I am in politics.

LADY UTTERWORD. I'm sure I beg your pardon. I never heard of you.

MANGAN. Let me tell you, Lady Utterword, that the Prime Minister of this country asked me to join the Government without even going through the nonsense of an election, as the dictator of a great public department.

LADY UTTERWORD. As a Conservative or a Liberal?

MANGAN. No such nonsense. As a practical business man. [*They all burst out laughing*]. What are you all laughing at?

MRS HUSHABYE. Oh, Alfred, Alfred!

ELLIE. You! who have to get my father to do everything for you!

MRS HUSHABYE. You! who are afraid of your own workmen!

HECTOR. You! with whom three women have been playing cat and mouse all the evening!

LADY UTTERWORD. You must have given an immense sum to the party funds, Mr Mangan.

MANGAN. Not a penny out of my own pocket. The syndicate found the money: they knew how useful I should be to them in the Government.

LADY UTTERWORD. This is most interesting and unexpected, Mr Mangan. And what have your administrative achievements been, so far?

MANGAN. Achievements? Well, I dont know what you call achievements; but Ive jolly well put a stop to the games of the other fellows in the other departments. Every man of them thought he was going to save the country all by himself, and do me out of the credit and out of my chance of a title. I took good care that if they wouldnt let me do it they shouldnt do it themselves either. I may not know anything about my own machinery; but I know how to stick a ramrod into the other fellow's. And now they all look the biggest fools going.

HECTOR. And in heaven's name, what do you look like?

MANGAN. I look like the fellow that was too clever for all the others, dont I? If that isnt a triumph of practical business, what is?

HECTOR. Is this England, or is it a madhouse?

LADY UTTERWORD. Do you expect to save the country, Mr Mangan?

MANGAN. Well, who else will? Will your Mr Randall save it?

LADY UTTERWORD. Randall the Rotter! Certainly not.

MANGAN. Will your brother-in-law save it with his moustache and his fine talk.

HECTOR. Yes, if they will let me.

MANGAN [sneering] Ah! Will they let you?

HECTOR. No. They prefer you.

MANGAN. Very well then, as youre in a world where I'm appreciated and youre not, youd best be civil to me, hadnt you? Who else is there but me?

LADY UTTERWORD. There is Hastings. Get rid of your ridiculous sham democracy; and give Hastings the necessary powers, and a good supply of bamboo to bring the British native to his senses: he will save the country with the greatest ease.

CAPTAIN SHOTOVER. It had better be lost. Any fool can govern with a stick in his hand. I could govern that way. It is not God's way. The man is a numskull.

LADY UTTERWORD. The man is worth all of you rolled into one. What do you say, Miss Dunn?

ELLIE. I think my father would do very well if people did not put upon him and cheat him and despise him because he is so good.

MANGAN [*contemptuously*] I think I see Mazzini Dunn getting into parliament or pushing his way into the Government. Weve not come to that yet, thank God! What do you say, Mrs Hushabye?

MRS HUSHABYE. Oh, *I* say it matters very little which of you governs the country so long as we govern you.

HECTOR. We? Who is we, pray?

MRS HUSHABYE. The devil's granddaughters, dear. The lovely women.

HECTOR [*raising his hands as before*] Fall, I say; and deliver us from the lures of Satan!

ELLIE. There seems to be nothing real in the world except my father and Shakespear. Marcus's tigers are false; Mr Mangan's millions are false; there is nothing really strong and true about Hesione but her beautiful black hair; and Lady Utterword's is too pretty to be real. The one thing that was left to me was the Captain's seventh degree of concentration: and that turns out to be –

CAPTAIN SHOTOVER. Rum.

LADY UTTERWORD [*placidly*] A good deal of my hair is quite genuine. The Duchess of Dithering offered me fifty guineas for this [*touching her forehead*] under the impression that it was a transformation; but it is all natural except the color.

MANGAN [*wildly*] Look here: I'm going to take off all my clothes [*he begins tearing off his coat*].

LADY UTTERWORD.		Mr Mangan!
CAPTAIN SHOTOVER.	[*in	Whats that?
HECTOR.	consternation*]	Ha! ha! Do. Do.
ELLIE.		Please dont.

MRS HUSHABYE [*catching his arm and stopping him*] Alfred: for shame! Are you mad?

MANGAN. Shame! What shame is there in this house? Let's all strip stark naked. We may as well do the thing thoroughly when we're about it. Weve stripped ourselves morally naked: well, let us strip ourselves physically naked as well, and see how we like it. I tell you I cant bear this. I was brought up to be respectable. I dont mind the women dyeing their hair and the men drinking: it's human nature. But it's not human nature to tell everybody about it. Every time one of you opens your mouth I go like this [*he cowers as if to avoid a missile*] afraid of what will come next. How are we to have any self-respect if we dont keep it up that we're better than we really are?

LADY UTTERWORD. I quite sympathize with you, Mr Mangan. I have been through it all; and I know by experience that men and women are delicate plants and must be cultivated under glass. Our family habit of throwing stones in all directions and letting the air in is not only unbearably rude, but positively dangerous. Still, there is no use catching physical colds as well as moral ones; so please keep your clothes on.

MANGAN. I'll do as I like: not what you tell me. Am I a child or a grown man? I wont stand this mothering tyranny. I'll go back to the city, where I'm respected and made much of.

MRS HUSHABYE. Goodbye, Alf. Think of us sometimes in the city. Think of Ellie's youth!

ELLIE. Think of Hesione's eyes and hair!

CAPTAIN SHOTOVER. Think of this garden in which you are not a dog barking to keep the truth out!

HECTOR. Think of Lady Utterword's beauty! her good sense! her style!

LADY UTTERWORD. Flatterer. Think, Mr Mangan, whether you can really do any better for yourself elsewhere: that is the essential point, isnt it?

MANGAN [*surrendering*] All right: all right. I'm done. Have it your own way. Only let me alone. I dont know whether I'm on my head or my heels when you all start on me like this. I'll stay. I'll marry her. I'll do anything for a quiet life. Are you satisfied now?

ELLIE. No. I never really intended to make you marry me, Mr Mangan. Never in the depths of my soul. I only wanted to feel my strength: to know that you could not escape if I chose to take you.

MANGAN [*indignantly*] What! Do you mean to say you are going to throw me over after my acting so handsome?

LADY UTTERWORD. I should not be too hasty, Miss Dunn. You can throw Mr Mangan over at any time up to the last moment. Very few men in his position go bankrupt. You can live very comfortably on his reputation for immense wealth.

ELLIE. I cannot commit bigamy, Lady Utterword.

MRS HUSHABYE.		Bigamy! Whatever on earth are you talking about, Ellie?
LADY UTTERWORD.	[*exclaiming all together*]	Bigamy! What do you mean, Miss Dunn?
MANGAN.		Bigamy! Do you mean to say youre married already?
HECTOR.		Bigamy! This is some enigma.

ELLIE. Only half an hour ago I became Captain Shotover's white wife.

MRS HUSHABYE. Ellie! What nonsense! Where?

ELLIE. In heaven, where all true marriages are made.

LADY UTTERWORD. Really, Miss Dunn! Really, papa!

MANGAN. He told me *I* was too old! And him a mummy!

HECTOR [*quoting Shelley*]

> Their altar the grassy earth outspread,
> And their priest the muttering wind.

ELLIE. Yes: I, Ellie Dunn, give my broken heart and my

strong sound soul to its natural captain, my spiritual husband and second father.

She draws the Captain's arm through hers, and pats his hand. The Captain remains fast asleep.

MRS HUSHABYE. Oh, thats very clever of you, pettikins. Very clever. Alfred: you could never have lived up to Ellie. You must be content with a little share of me.

MANGAN [*sniffing and wiping his eyes*] It isnt kind – [*his emotion chokes him*].

LADY UTTERWORD. You are well out of it, Mr Mangan. Miss Dunn is the most conceited young woman I have met since I came back to England.

MRS HUSHABYE. Oh, Ellie isnt conceited. Are you, pettikins?

ELLIE. I know my strength now, Hesione.

MANGAN. Brazen, I call you. Brazen.

MRS HUSHABYE. Tut tut, Alfred: dont be rude. Dont you feel how lovely this marriage night is, made in heaven? Arnt you happy, you and Hector? Open your eyes: Addy and Ellie look beautiful enough to please the most fastidious man: we live and love and have not a care in the world. We women have managed all that for you. Why in the name of common sense do you go on as if you were two miserable wretches?

CAPTAIN SHOTOVER. I tell you happiness is no good. You can be happy when you are only half alive. I am happier now I am half dead than ever I was in my prime. But there is no blessing on my happiness.

ELLIE [*her face lighting up*] Life with a blessing! that is what I want. Now I know the real reason why I couldnt marry Mr Mangan: there would be no blessing on our marriage. There is a blessing on my broken heart. There is a blessing on your beauty, Hesione. There is a blessing on your father's spirit. Even on the lies of Marcus there is a blessing; but on Mr Mangan's money there is none.

MANGAN. I dont understand a word of that.

ELLIE. Neither do I. But I know it means something.

MANGAN. Dont say there was any difficulty about the blessing. I was ready to get a bishop to marry us.

MRS HUSHABYE. Isnt he a fool, pettikins?

HECTOR [*fiercely*] Do not scorn the man. We are all fools.

Mazzini, in pyjamas and a richly colored silk dressing-gown, comes from the house, on Lady Utterword's side.

MRS HUSHABYE. Oh! here comes the only man who ever resisted me. Whats the matter, Mr Dunn? Is the house on fire?

MAZZINI. Oh no: nothing's the matter; but really it's impossible to go to sleep with such an interesting conversation going on under one's window, and on such a beautiful night too. I just had to come down and join you all. What has it all been about?

MRS HUSHABYE. Oh, wonderful things, soldier of freedom.

HECTOR. For example, Mangan, as a practical business man, has tried to undress himself and has failed ignominiously; whilst you, as an idealist, have succeeded brilliantly.

MAZZINI. I hope you dont mind my being like this, Mrs Hushabye. [*He sits down on the campstool*].

MRS HUSHABYE. On the contrary, I could wish you always like that.

LADY UTTERWORD. Your daughter's match is off, Mr Dunn. It seems that Mr Mangan, whom we all supposed to be a man of property, owns absolutely nothing.

MAZZINI. Well of course I knew that, Lady Utterword. But if people believe in him and are always giving him money, whereas they dont believe in me and never give me any, how can I ask poor Ellie to depend on what I can do for her?

MANGAN. Dont you run away with this idea that I have nothing. I –

HECTOR. Oh, dont explain. We understand. You have a couple of thousand pounds in exchequer bills, 50,000 shares worth tenpence a dozen, and half a dozen tabloids of cyanide of potassium to poison yourself with when you are found out. Thats the reality of your millions.

MAZZINI. Oh no, no, no. He is quite honest: the businesses are genuine and perfectly legal.

HECTOR [*disgusted*] Yah! Not even a great swindler!

MANGAN. So you think. But Ive been too many for some honest men for all that.

LADY UTTERWORD. There is no pleasing you, Mr Mangan. You are determined to be neither rich nor poor, honest nor dishonest.

MANGAN. There you go again. Ever since I came into this silly house I have been made to look like a fool, though I'm as good a man in this house as in the city.

ELLIE [*musically*] Yes: this silly house, this strangely happy house, this agonizing house, this house without foundations. I shall call it Heartbreak House.

MRS HUSHABYE. Stop, Ellie; or I shall howl like an animal.

MANGAN [*breaks into a low snivelling*]!!!

MRS HUSHABYE. There! you have set Alfred off.

ELLIE. I like him best when he is howling.

CAPTAIN SHOTOVER. Silence! [*Mangan subsides into silence*]. I say, let the heart break in silence.

HECTOR. Do you accept that name for your house?

CAPTAIN SHOTOVER. It is not my house: it is only my kennel.

HECTOR. We have been too long here. We do not live in this house: we haunt it.

LADY UTTERWORD [*heart torn*] It is dreadful to think how you have been here all these years while I have gone round the world. I escaped young; but it has drawn me back. It wants to break my heart too. But it shant. I have left you and it behind. It was silly of me to come back. I felt sentimental about papa and Hesione and the old place. I felt them calling to me.

MAZZINI. But what a very natural and kindly and charming human feeling, Lady Utterword!

LADY UTTERWORD. So I thought, Mr Dunn. But I know now that it was only the last of my influenza. I found that I was not remembered and not wanted.

CAPTAIN SHOTOVER. You left because you did not want us. Was there no heartbreak in that for your father? You tore yourself up by the roots; and the ground healed up and brought forth fresh plants and forgot you. What right had you to come back and probe old wounds?

MRS HUSHABYE. You were a complete stranger to me at first, Addy; but now I feel as if you had never been away.

LADY UTTERWORD. Thank you, Hesione; but the influenza is quite cured. The place may be Heartbreak House to you, Miss Dunn, and to this gentleman from the city who seems to have so little self-control; but to me it is only a very ill-regulated and rather untidy villa without any stables.

HECTOR. Inhabited by – ?

ELLIE. A crazy old sea captain and a young singer who adores him.

MRS HUSHABYE. A sluttish female, trying to stave off a double chin and an elderly spread, vainly wooing a born soldier of freedom.

MAZZINI. Oh, really, Mrs Hushabye –

MANGAN. A member of His Majesty's Government that everybody sets down as a nincompoop: dont forget him, Lady Utterword.

LADY UTTERWORD. And a very fascinating gentleman whose chief occupation is to be married to my sister.

HECTOR. All heartbroken imbeciles.

MAZZINI. Oh no. Surely, if I may say so, rather a favorable specimen of what is best in our English culture. You are very charming people, most advanced, unprejudiced, frank, humane, unconventional, democratic, free-thinking, and everything that is delightful to thoughtful people.

MRS HUSHABYE. You do us proud, Mazzini.

MAZZINI. I am not flattering, really. Where else could I feel perfectly at ease in my pyjamas? I sometimes dream that I am in very distinguished society, and suddenly I have nothing on but my pyjamas! Sometimes I havnt even pyjamas. And I always feel overwhelmed with confusion. But here, I dont mind in the least: it seems quite natural.

LADY UTTERWORD. An infallible sign that you are not now in really distinguished society, Mr Dunn. If you were in my house, you would feel embarrassed.

MAZZINI. I shall take particular care to keep out of your house, Lady Utterword.

LADY UTTERWORD. You will be quite wrong, Mr Dunn. I should make you very comfortable; and you would not have the trouble and anxiety of wondering whether you should wear your purple and gold or your green and crimson dressing-gown at dinner. You complicate life instead of simplifying it by doing these ridiculous things.

ELLIE. Your house is not Heartbreak House: is it, Lady Utterword?

HECTOR. Yet she breaks hearts, easy as her house is. That poor devil upstairs with his flute howls when she twists his heart, just as Mangan howls when my wife twists his.

LADY UTTERWORD. That is because Randall has nothing to do but have his heart broken. It is a change from having his head shampooed. Catch anyone breaking Hastings' heart!

CAPTAIN SHOTOVER. The numskull wins, after all.

LADY UTTERWORD. I shall go back to my numskull with the greatest satisfaction when I am tired of you all, clever as you are.

MANGAN [*huffily*] I never set up to be clever.

LADY UTTERWORD. I forgot you, Mr Mangan.

MANGAN. Well, I dont see that quite, either.

LADY UTTERWORD. You may not be clever, Mr Mangan; but you are successful.

MANGAN. But I dont want to be regarded merely as a successful man. I have an imagination like anyone else. I have a presentiment –

MRS HUSHABYE. Oh, you are impossible, Alfred. Here I am devoting myself to you; and you think of nothing but your ridiculous presentiment. You bore me. Come and talk poetry to me under the stars. [*She drags him away into the darkness*].

MANGAN [*tearfully, as he disappears*] Yes: it's all very well to make fun of me; but if you only knew –

HECTOR [*impatiently*] How is all this going to end?

MAZZINI. It wont end, Mr Hushabye. Life doesnt end: it goes on.

ELLIE. Oh, it cant go on for ever. I'm always expecting something. I dont know what it is; but life must come to a point sometime.

LADY UTTERWORD. The point for a young woman of your age is a baby.

HECTOR. Yes, but damn it, I have the same feeling; and *I* cant have a baby.

LADY UTTERWORD. By deputy, Hector.

HECTOR. But I have children. All that is over and done with for me: and yet I too feel that this cant last. We sit here talking, and leave everything to Mangan and to chance and to the devil. Think of the powers of destruction that Mangan and his mutual admiration gang wield! It's madness: it's like giving a torpedo to a badly brought up child to play at earthquakes with.

MAZZINI. I know. I used often to think about that when I was young.

HECTOR. Think! Whats the good of thinking about it? Why didnt you do something?

MAZZINI. But I did. I joined societies and made speeches and wrote pamphlets. That was all I could do. But, you know, though the people in the societies thought they knew more than Mangan, most of them wouldnt have joined if they had known as much. You see they had never had any money to handle or any men to manage. Every year I expected a revolution, or some frightful smash-up: it seemed impossible that we could blunder and muddle on any longer. But nothing happened, except, of course, the usual poverty and crime and drink that we are used to. Nothing ever does happen. It's amazing how well we get along, all things considered.

LADY UTTERWORD. Perhaps, somebody cleverer than you and Mr Mangan was at work all the time.

MAZZINI. Perhaps so. Though I was brought up not to believe in anything, I often feel that there is a great deal to be said for the theory of an overruling Providence, after all.

LADY UTTERWORD. Providence! I meant Hastings.

MAZZINI. Oh, I beg your pardon, Lady Utterword.

CAPTAIN SHOTOVER. Every drunken skipper trusts to Providence. But one of the ways of Providence with drunken skippers is to run them on the rocks.

MAZZINI. Very true, no doubt, at sea. But in politics, I assure you, they only run into jellyfish. Nothing happens.

CAPTAIN SHOTOVER. At sea nothing happens to the sea. Nothing happens to the sky. The sun comes up from the east and goes down to the west. The moon grows from a sickle to an arc lamp, and comes later and later until she is lost in the light as other things are lost in the darkness. After the typhoon, the flying-fish glitter in the sunshine like birds. It's amazing how they get along, all things considered. Nothing happens, except something not worth mentioning.

ELLIE. What is that, O Captain, my captain?

CAPTAIN SHOTOVER [*savagely*] Nothing but the smash of the drunken skipper's ship on the rocks, the splintering of her rotten timbers, the tearing of her rusty plates, the drowning of the crew like rats in a trap.

ELLIE. Moral: dont take rum.

CAPTAIN SHOTOVER [*vehemently*] That is a lie, child. Let a man drink ten barrels of rum a day, he is not a drunken skipper until he is a drifting skipper. Whilst he can lay his course and stand on his bridge and steer it, he is no drunkard. It is the man who lies drinking in his bunk and trusts to Providence that I call the drunken skipper, though he drank nothing but the waters of the River Jordan.

ELLIE. Splendid! And you havnt had a drop for an hour. You see you dont need it: your own spirit is not dead.

CAPTAIN SHOTOVER. Echoes: nothing but echoes. The last shot was fired years ago.

HECTOR. And this ship we are all in? This soul's prison we call England?

CAPTAIN SHOTOVER. The captain is in his bunk, drinking bottled ditch-water; and the crew is gambling in the forecastle. She will strike and sink and split. Do you think the laws of God will be suspended in favor of England because you were born in it?

HECTOR. Well, I dont mean to be drowned like a rat in a trap. I still have the will to live. What am I to do?

CAPTAIN SHOTOVER. Do? Nothing simpler. Learn your business as an Englishman.

HECTOR. And what may my business as an Englishman be, pray?

CAPTAIN SHOTOVER. Navigation. Learn it and live; or leave it and be damned.

ELLIE. Quiet, quiet; youll tire yourself.

MAZZINI. I thought all that once, Captain; but I assure you nothing will happen.

A dull distant explosion is heard.

HECTOR [*starting up*] What was that?

CAPTAIN SHOTOVER. Something happening [*he blows his whistle*]. Breakers ahead!

The light goes out.

HECTOR [*furiously*] Who put that light out? Who dared put that light out?

NURSE GUINNESS [*running in from the house to the middle of the esplanade*] I did, sir. The police have telephoned to say we'll be summoned if we dont put that light out: it can be seen for miles.

HECTOR. It shall be seen for a hundred miles [*he dashes into the house*].

NURSE GUINNESS. The rectory is nothing but a heap of bricks, they say. Unless we can give the rector a bed he has nowhere to lay his head this night.

CAPTAIN SHOTOVER. The Church is on the rocks, breaking up. I told him it would unless it headed for God's open sea.

NURSE GUINNESS. And you are all to go down to the cellars.

CAPTAIN SHOTOVER. Go there yourself, you and all the crew. Batten down the hatches.

NURSE GUINNESS. And hide beside the coward I married! I'll go on the roof first. [*The lamp lights up again*]. There! Mr Hushabye's turned it on again.

THE BURGLAR [*hurrying in and appealing to Nurse Guinness*] Here: wheres the way to that gravel pit? The boot-boy says theres a cave in the gravel pit. Them cellars is no use. Wheres the gravel pit, Captain?

NURSE GUINNESS. Go straight on past the flagstaff until you fall into it and break your dirty neck. [*She pushes him contemptuously towards the flagstaff, and herself goes to the foot of the hammock and waits there, as it were by Ariadne's cradle*].

Another and louder explosion is heard. The burglar stops and stands trembling.

ELLIE [*rising*] That was nearer.

CAPTAIN SHOTOVER. The next one will get us. [*He rises*]. Stand by, all hands, for judgment.

THE BURGLAR. Oh my Lordy God! [*He rushes away frantically past the flagstaff into the gloom*].

MRS HUSHABYE [*emerging panting from the darkness*] Who was that running away? [*She comes to Ellie*]. Did you hear the explosions? And the sound in the sky: it's splendid: it's like an orchestra: it's like Beethoven.

ELLIE. By thunder, Hesione: it is Beethoven.

She and Hesione throw themselves into one another's arms in wild excitement. The light increases.

MAZZINI [*anxiously*] The light is getting brighter.

NURSE GUINNESS [*looking up at the house*] It's Mr Hushabye turning on all the lights in the house and tearing down the curtains.

RANDALL [*rushing in in his pyjamas, distractedly waving a flute*] Ariadne: my soul, my precious, go down to the cellars: I beg and implore you, go down to the cellars!

LADY UTTERWORD [*quite composed in her hammock*] The governor's wife in the cellars with the servants! Really, Randall!

RANDALL. But what shall I do if you are killed?

LADY UTTERWORD. You will probably be killed, too, Randall. Now play your flute to shew that you are not afraid; and be good. Play us Keep the home fires burning.

NURSE GUINNESS [*grimly*] Theyll keep the home fires burning for us: them up there.

RANDALL [*having tried to play*] My lips are trembling. I cant get a sound.

MAZZINI. I hope poor Mangan is safe.

MRS HUSHABYE. He is hiding in the cave in the gravel pit.

CAPTAIN SHOTOVER. My dynamite drew him there. It is the hand of God.

HECTOR [*returning from the house and striding across to his for-*

mer place] There is not half light enough. We should be blazing to the skies.

ELLIE [*tense with excitement*] Set fire to the house, Marcus.

MRS HUSHABYE. My house! No.

HECTOR. I thought of that; but it would not be ready in time.

CAPTAIN SHOTOVER. The judgment has come. Courage will not save you; but it will shew that your souls are still alive.

MRS HUSHABYE. Sh-sh! Listen: do you hear it now? It's magnificent.

They all turn away from the house and look up, listening.

HECTOR [*gravely*] Miss Dunn: you can do no good here. We of this house are only moths flying into the candle. You had better go down to the cellar.

ELLIE [*scornfully*] I dont think.

MAZZINI. Ellie, dear, there is no disgrace in going to the cellar. An officer would order his soldiers to take cover. Mr Hushabye is behaving like an amateur. Mangan and the burglar are acting very sensibly; and it is they who will survive.

ELLIE. Let them. I shall behave like an amateur. But why should you run any risk?

MAZZINI. Think of the risk those poor fellows up there are running!

NURSE GUINNESS. Think of them, indeed, the murdering blackguards! What next?

A terrific explosion shakes the earth. They reel back into their seats, or clutch the nearest support. They hear the falling of the shattered glass from the windows.

MAZZINI. Is anyone hurt?

HECTOR. Where did it fall?

NURSE GUINNESS [*in hideous triumph*] Right in the gravel pit: I seen it. Serve un right! I seen it [*she runs away towards the gravel pit, laughing harshly*].

HECTOR. One husband gone.

CAPTAIN SHOTOVER. Thirty pounds of good dynamite wasted.

MAZZINI. Oh, poor Mangan!

HECTOR. Are you immortal that you need pity him? Our turn next.

They wait in silence and intense expectation. Hesione and Ellie hold each other's hand tight.

A distant explosion is heard.

MRS HUSHABYE [*relaxing her grip*] Oh! they have passed us.

LADY UTTERWORD. The danger is over, Randall. Go to bed.

CAPTAIN SHOTOVER. Turn in, all hands. The ship is safe. [*He sits down and goes asleep*].

ELLIE [*disappointedly*] Safe!

HECTOR [*disgustedly*] Yes, safe. And how damnably dull the world has become again suddenly! [*He sits down*].

MAZZINI [*sitting down*] I was quite wrong, after all. It is we who have survived; and Mangan and the burglar –

HECTOR. – the two burglars –

LADY UTTERWORD. – the two practical men of business –

MAZZINI. – both gone. And the poor clergyman will have to get a new house.

MRS HUSHABYE. But what a glorious experience! I hope they'll come again tomorrow night.

ELLIE [*radiant at the prospect*] Oh, I hope so.

Randall at last succeeds in keeping the home fires burning on his flute.